W9-BEF-995

All of the author's proceeds from sales or
donations of this book benefit the

SARA & SAM SCHOFFER
HOLOCAUST RESOURCE CENTER
THE RICHARD STOCKTON COLLEGE OF NEW JERSEY

Donations may be mailed to:
Sara & Sam Schoffer Holocaust Resource Center
P.O Box 195 • Pomona, NJ 08240
(609)-652-4699

Two Voices:
A Mother & Son,
Holocaust Survivors

Donald (Chipkin) Berkman

and Maryann McLoughlin

A Project of The Richard Stockton College of New Jersey
Sam and Sara Schoffer Holocaust Resource Center
and Graphics Production

COMTEQ™
PUBLISHING

MARGATE, NEW JERSEY

STOCKTON COLLEGE
THE RICHARD STOCKTON COLLEGE OF NEW JERSEY

NEW JERSEY'S
GREEN COLLEGE®
Stockton College is an AA/EO institution.

Published by:

ComteQ Publishing

A division of ComteQ Communications, LLC

101 N. Washington Ave. • Suite 2B

Margate, New Jersey 08402

609-487-9000 • Fax 609-487-9099

Email: publisher@comtcqpublishing.com

Website: www.ComteQpublishing.com

ISBN 978-1-935232-15-5

Library of Congress Control Number 2009942940

Book/Cover Design by Sarah Messina, Stockton Graphics Production

Endnotes and Discussion Questions by Maryann McLoughlin

Printed in the United States of America

10 9 8 7 6 5 4 3 2 1

In memory of
the million and a half children
murdered in the Holocaust.
My guilt is that I survived to tell my story.
Their stories are forever untold!

Acknowledgement

My thanks and love to my wife, Nan, who always listens to and hears the stories of our horrible lives during the war.

I want also to thank The Richard Stockton College of New Jersey for being so extraordinarily involved with Holocaust education. From the President of Stockton, Dr. Herman J. Saatkamp, to the Dean of General Studies, Dr. G. Jan Colijn, and the Director of the Holocaust Resource Center, Gail H. Rosenthal, they have honored their commitment to the education mission of the Holocaust Center and to all the Holocaust survivors—adults and children—who, however resilient, struggle, every day, with the pain and other residual effects of our Holocaust experiences.

I am especially grateful to Dr. Maryann McLoughlin for her efforts to hear the two voices, the mother's and the child's, the older and the younger, telling about our lives, hiding in the forests, during the years 1942 to 1945, as well as about our lives in poverty and deprivation for many years after the Holocaust until our eventual triumph.

My mother's life in the United States was blessed by her children: me and my wife Nan, daughters Sarah (David), Zelda (Danny) and Riva (Kevin); her grandchildren: Joel, Robin, Alan, Michelle, Steve (Vita), Beatty (Joe), Bobby (Cheryl) Anne (Albert), Janice (Lennie), Michael and Mathew; and by her great-grandchildren: Logan, Chloe, Mason, Sara, Lanie, Michal, Elanit, Jacob, Rebecca, Hannah, Eitan, Leah, Gabby, Eli, Denah, Aaron, Naomi, Arianna, and Eve.

Most of all, my love and thanks to my mother, Sara, who for three years was my loving protector and companion. Dressed in tatters, hungry, cold, friendless, she persevered, determined that we would survive to bear witness and to embrace life again.

Donald Berkman

Under a futile *Torah*
Under an imprisoned star
Your mother gave birth to you.

—From "Both Your Mothers," Jerry Ficowski

Table of Contents

Sara Berkman Chipkin's testimony is taken from a *Shoah* Foundation interview done by Taffy Gould, in Miami Beach, Florida, on December 19, 1995.

Preface

Courageous, wise, humorous, resourceful, and family-oriented—these words describe my mother-in-law, Sara Baron Berkman Chipkin. She was a young woman alone in the woods with a toddler, continually vigilant and brave, struggling to keep her son safe.

Sara was the essence of a survivor. Was it her will power, a sixth sense, her intelligence, a mother's boundless love? Perhaps it was all of these. Perhaps it was her determination that at least the two of them—mother and son—would survive the killing fields of Ponar, despite the loss of her husband, mother-in-law, sisters, brothers, nieces, and nephews. On and on, until forty-nine members of her family, including aunts, uncles, and first cousins were murdered.

The loves she lost were with her every day. A smell, a flower, an expression, anything at all would evoke memories of these beloved ones. We heard her stories every day; she was desperate to share them and desperate for us to be aware of the existence of her lost family. She wanted those murdered to live on in us. And they do.

My mother-in law was honored by her community as a Holocaust survivor, so the pain of her losses and her experiences were validated in many ways.

On the other hand, child survivors of the Holocaust have often been overlooked. Despite this, Don has been a generous supporter of Holocaust education, providing scholarships for many teachers and graduate students. He is also supporting programming at the Jewish Community Center about child survivors of the Holocaust.

Don is generous with his time as well, often speaking to students about his Holocaust experiences.

Despite his bitterness over his lost childhood and loss of family, Don is a loving man and a good man. Yet he continues to struggle with the pain of his memories and his experiences, without the consolation that sharing the massive trauma would bring.

I believe that writing his memoir will bring him some consolation and provide a catharsis of sorts.

Nan Berkman

Editor's Preface

It seems strange that some survivors of the Holocaust, a genocide that began with the exclusion of certain groups from the community and ended with their exclusion from their country and finally from this world, would exclude child survivors from the survivor community. By doing this they are effectively ignoring child survivors' experiences, memories, and pain.

Psychologists agree that mourning is enhanced by joining forces with others from a historical event [the Holocaust]. But child survivors are generally barred from joining forces with other survivors. Fogelman and Bass-Wichelhaus point out that when older survivors reminisce, child survivors are often told, "Oh, what do you remember? You were too young." Remarks such as these "serve to alienate and isolate child survivors and to suppress their memories" . . . . In general, according to Fogelman and Bass-Wichelhaus, "Holocaust child survivors have been known to have their pain and suffering *in*validated" (35). Thus, child survivors have formed their own organization called N.A.H.O.S., the National Association of Jewish Child Holocaust Survivors, Inc. The group has moved from dependency to goal-oriented action; for example, members have challenged the German reparation system (39).

Still isolated in this group of child Holocaust survivors are the hidden children; they feel that their experiences have not been "as validated" as those surviving in ghettos and camps (40). Therefore, the ADL Hidden Child Foundation, a self-help movement for hidden children was founded in 1991 (43).

Fogelman and Bass-Wichelhaus write:

> With some exceptions, children survived the Holocaust in isolation. The isolation continued in the post-liberation years because they were not encouraged, and often dissuaded, from sharing their massive trauma. The majority of group experiences allows for diverse motivations to be met. Some are just curious to meet others from a similar background and socialize, while others feel a need to work through the emotional conflicts that have resulted from their persecution and losses. (46)

When I compare my childhood with Donald Berkman's, I have no doubt that Don is truly a Holocaust survivor. We were born in the same year; Don was born in the beginning of 1941, in January, and I was born at the end of 1941, in December. There the similarities end. For I lived in a warm and cozy home surrounded by my parents, grandparents, aunts, uncles, and cousins. Don lived in the forest; he was cold, and his extended family had been murdered at Ponar. I had plenty to eat, and milk and water to drink, and I had clothing that was not ragged. Don drank the dew from leaves, and it was a lucky day if he had milk to drink. I never saw a dead body as Don did when he was four or five years old. I never felt the anxiety and fear he must have felt when he had to hide in the forest, in an attic, in a warming oven, or in a pit covered with leaves.

When I was old enough for school, I went to our local community kindergarten; when Don was old enough for school, he was in the Displaced Persons Camp; school was not there for him. It was not until he was nine years old and an immigrant to the U. S. that he was placed into kindergarten. My language was English from my birth; Don heard many languages in his short life in Europe but had to learn English in the U. S. when he was eight years old. Easier for children, this is true; however, it is still disorienting to be immersed in a new language. On and on, the contrasts proliferate.

To this day, Don's trauma continues; he still has nightmares and is frequently reminded of the Holocaust and what he lost. Moreover, he still feels guilt because he, unlike most Jewish children, did survive.

I am honored to work on this memoir with Don. I hope the process of writing about his mother and his experiences will help bring him some consolation.

Maryann McLoughlin
Holocaust Resource Center
The Richard Stockton College of New Jersey

Editor's Note

This memoir is told in two voices: the voice of the mother and the voice of the son. Therefore, there is some repetition as each relates the past. I thought, however, that it was important to hear both voices tell about their experiences during the Holocaust and after.

Maryann McLoughlin

Maps

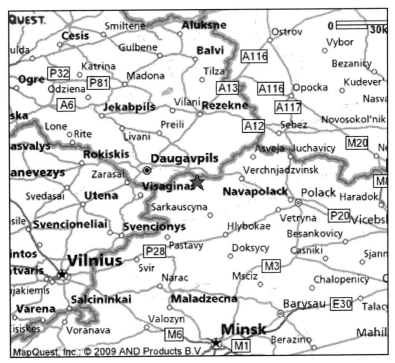

Druysk, location marked with a star, is the shtetl where Sara and her family lived
until 1941.

Krāslava, Latvia starred, where Sara was sent after her mother died. See Druysk (Drujsk) circled.

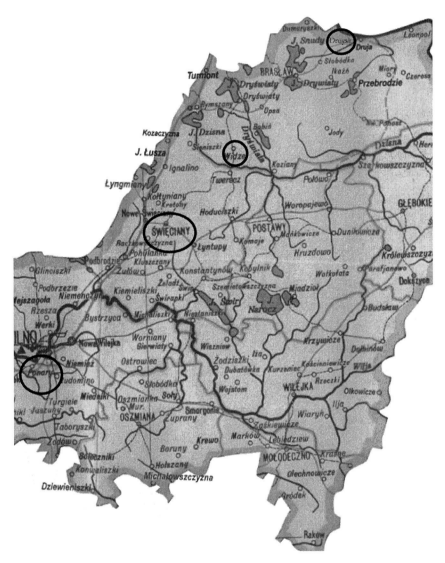

Yosel Berkman and family as well as other citizens of Druysk were taken to several ghettos: Widze (Vidzy) and Swieciany before they were murdered in Ponar (Ponary), near Vilna (Wilno). Note the trajectory of their journey.

Chapter 1-6 Mother's Voice

Mother's Voice
Chapter 1

1910 This was a remarkable year. In January of 1910, the brightest comet of the twentieth century appeared, outshining the planet Venus—The Great Daylight Comet of 1910, whose brilliance was visible in broad daylight. On April 20, 1910, another comet, Halley's Comet, made a close approach to Earth—a spectacular sight, heightening the delight of astronomers when on May 18, 1910, the Earth passed through the tail of this comet. Legend has it that the comet brought destruction.

I was born on May 15, 1910, between the time Halley's Comet was first sighted and the time when the Earth went through the comet's tail. I was born Chaisorel (Hebrew name, Sara) Baron in Druysk, a suburb of Vilna, Lithuania, called Vilna Gubernia, then part of the Russian Empire.[1] Druysk did not need Halley's Comet to bring it devastation; belonging to the Russian Empire was enough. Lithuania had been "devastated, robbed, and oppressed for centuries" (Kasaty).

Until 1930, Druysk was part of the Russian Empire. In 1930, Druysk became part of Poland. In 1939, under the Nazi-Soviet Pact, a part of the U.S.S.R. until 1990 when Belarus and Lithuania gained independence, borders were remade, and Druysk became part of Belarus. ("Druysk, Belarus")

My *shtetl* (a small town), Druysk was eleven miles southwest of Brasław, Poland, and twelve miles north-northwest of Krāslavia, Latvia. The townspeople in Druysk were Jews. Our *shtetl* was surrounded by Christians, but in our town all were Jews, so we had not experienced pogroms. There was one woman and her son who were non-Jewish. They helped Jewish families on the Sabbath by lighting candles and stoves, something religiously forbidden on the Sabbath.

Jews had their own land. In our town we had a couple of rich people, a few middle-class, and a lot of poor people. The rich were not rich like American rich but rich compared to the rest of the people in the *shtetl*. The Jews were orthodox but not extreme like the Hasidic with their white stockings and *tzitzit* (fringes or tassels).[2] Jews of Druysk did not work on the Sabbath. We were a close knit community. We were called *Mitnagdim* (or opponents) and followed the Vilna Gaon, who was opposed to Hasidism.[3] We had two synagogues—the larger was Ashkenazi; the other was Hasidic but Lithuanian Hasidic. They did not wear black clothing nor ear locks (*payos*). We lived in a little house, with a dirt floor and no electricity or running water. There was an outhouse behind the house and a well in the front of the house.

My father was a businessman and also a rabbi who was in a partnership with his brother-in-law, his sister's husband. They sold geese to the Germans and flax to Russia and Latvia.[4] The flax was sold for material. Flax fiber, "soft, lustrous and flexible, was extracted from the bast or skin of the stem of the flax plant, which is stronger than cotton fiber but less elastic. The best grades of flax were used for linen fabrics such as damasks, lace, and sheeting." ("Flax")

My father had been married three times and had four children from his first wife, four from his second wife (his first wife's sister), and one child from his third wife. I was one of the daughters of the second wife. My mother died in 1912 when I was two years old, so I don't know anything about her. Before she died she had given birth to two sons and two daughters. One brother was four years older than I. Then I had a second brother and a younger sister, Frumka Malka.

In 1914, when I was four years old, World War I started, and Belarus became "a battlefield." Nearby Vilna was occupied by the Germans, while Minsk "remained under the Russians." Communications between different parts of Belarus became problematic (Kasaty).

During the war, in 1916, my father became ill with the flu sickness.[5] I remember one night when I was six years old; around this time I was sleeping in my father's bed when he passed away from flu. I did not know he had died. After my father's death, I was sent to live with my father's sister in Krāslava, Latvia.

Because of my young age and my own problems, I was not aware that 1917 was an important year historically to Belarus. Kasaty explains:

> The revolutions of 1917 in Russia first drove away the tsarist bureaucrats from the "Russian" part of Belarus, but in October they were replaced by Bolsheviks. With this unstable political situation all the Belarusian public organizations gathered in the All-Belarusian Congress, the purpose of which was to decide the political future of Belarus. The Congress decided to proclaim the autonomous Belarusian Democratic Republic, but this was disbanded by the Bolsheviks.

By 1930, Druysk was a part of Poland.

Mother's Voice
Chapter 2

After my father died, we were very poor. The family had to decide who would raise us. We had no grandparents to go to. My mother's side of the family was good to us, and my mother's sister was nice, but she was not able to take us. My brothers were sent all over. My younger sister, Frumka Malka, went to an uncle's home. I never knew what happened to the first four children of my father. I never saw them again. Baby Esther, my stepsister, the daughter of my father's third wife, stayed with her mother in Druysk. I was sent to Latvia to live with my father's sister who had fourteen children; her husband had been my father's business partner.

My aunt and uncle lived in Krāslava, Latvia, a city, not a *shtetl*, twelve miles north northwest of Druysk.[6] The family was comfortable. I wasn't. I was a servant in their house helping take care of the fourteen children. I became a slave to my aunt's children, my cousins, for eight years, until I was fourteen. Every day I had to clean the house and care for the children. They were unkind to me. I could not play outside even though there were lots of children. With my work, I had no time to play.

My cousins went to school. My aunt gave me one piece of paper, but I was not allowed to attend school, except for one day.

In fact, my cousins were in a school that the United States built for them. A cousin who had immigrated to the United States came back to visit his parents and saw how it was—poor compared to the U.S. The school room was in a house. They learned Hebrew and Polish.

In 1924, when I was fourteen, after eight years at my aunt's, I returned to Druysk, to my father's house. I had gone back to Druysk to visit my brothers, and I never returned to my aunt's in Krāslava, Latvia.

Mother's Voice
Chapter 3

When I came back to Druysk in 1924, I needed to earn money. I decided to have a business, buying and selling. I went to the non-Jews, the Christians, and they sold me something and then I sold that in my little town. Or I bought in my town and then went outside the town to sell this to the Christians. In the end, I had a very good business. By us I was rich; like the U.S., no. Mostly I worked but we did have dancing on Saturday night after the Sabbath had ended. One person played the fiddle.

In 1928, when I was eighteen years old, I married Yosel Berkman. I had known him for a long time. He also lived in Druysk. Yosel was a shoemaker, a maker of soles.[7] His business was not very good because the town was small, and people didn't often need new soles. Yosel liked to smoke, but he could not afford tobacco, so he went into the forest, gathered leaves from the forest floor, crushed them, and mixed these leaves with a little tobacco and smoked that.

Yosel's mother, Shana, lived with us. Her husband had died young, so she was all alone. We had a wonderful relationship.

In 1933, after five years of marriage, Yosel and I had a son, delivered by the midwife, but he died shortly after childbirth. Our son, Chaim Hirsch, was born in 1941, after I had been married for thirteen years.

When Hitler came to power in 1933, we heard rumors about what he was doing to the Jews, but we didn't believe them. I never knew anything about *Kristallnacht*, The November Pogrom of 1938.[8]

In 1939 when the Germans attacked Poland, Soviet soldiers came to Druysk. At that time the Soviets and Germans were allies because of the Nazi-Soviet Pact of August 1939, when Germany and the Soviets agreed on a non-aggression pact as well as agreeing to the partition of Poland.[9] One brother and my husband were taken into the army at this time, so I could not flee East as some did. We could not go anyplace.

My sister, Frumka Malka, returned Vilna; she walked to Druysk with her two daughters. She did not like the Communist regime in Vilna.

The Soviets restricted public religious life, nationalized businesses, and collected workers into cooperatives. Some people were exiled to Siberia. The Soviets did not persecute the Jews, however. For the next two years we lived peacefully.

Then, on June 22, 1941, six months after our son, Chaim Hirsch, was born, the Germans broke the non-aggression pact, first attacking Soviet-occupied Poland. This was called Operation Barbarossa.[10] The Soviets immediately left Druysk and the surrounding areas, ahead of Field Marshal Ernst Busch's Sixteenth Army's advance into the Vilna area of Poland.[11]

> The *Holocaust Encyclopedia* explains:
>
> Before the outbreak of World War II, the city of Vilna was part of northeastern Poland. [However,] under the terms of the German-Soviet Pact, Vilna, along with the rest of eastern Poland, was occupied by Soviet forces in late September 1939. In October 1939, the Soviet Union transferred the Vilna region to Lithuania. The population of the city was 200,000 at this time, including over 55,000 Jews. In addition, some 12,000-15,000 Jewish refugees from

German-occupied Poland found refuge in the city. Soviet forces occupied Lithuania in June 1940, and in August 1940 incorporated Vilna, along with the rest of Lithuania, into the Soviet Union. On June 22, 1941, Germany attacked Soviet forces in Eastern Europe. The German army occupied Vilna on June 24, 1941, the third day after the invasion. . . . .

By the end of 1941, the Einsatzgruppen had killed about 40,000 Jews in Ponary. ("Vilna")

Vilna was not the only city where Jews were killed: "Within six months of the German occupation of Kovno, the Germans and their Lithuania collaborators had murdered half of the Jews in Kovno" ("Kovno").[12] At least 5,000 Lithuanian Jews of Kovno, largely taken from the city's Jewish ghetto, were transported to the Ninth Fort and killed. According to the *Holocaust Encyclopedia* "German mobile killing units, *Einsatzgruppe* detachments and Lithuanian auxiliaries shot thousands of Jewish men, women, and children, primarily in the Ninth Fort, but also in the Fourth and Seventh Forts" ("Kovno")[13]

In addition, Jews from as far as France, Austria and Germany were brought to Kovno during the Nazi occupation and executed in the Ninth Fort. In 1944, as the Soviets moved in, the Germans liquidated the ghetto and what had by then come to be known as the "Fort of Death," and the prisoners, most skilled workers, were dispersed to other camps. Many were sent to Estonia to a concentration camp called Klooga, opened in 1943. During the final days with the Soviets advancing into Estonia, prisoners were evacuated. Most of the remaining prisoners at Klooga were then shot by Nazi guards; their bodies were stacked like logs onto wooden pyres, kerosene was poured on them, and they were burnt. On September 28, 1944, when the Soviets reached Klooga only about eighty-five of 2,400 left after the evacuation were alive. ("Kovno")

"From 1941 to 1944, the German occupation of Lithuania area resulted in the deaths of 2.2 million people, the destruction of 209 cities and townships, and 9,200 villages, and uncounted material losses" ("Belarus").

In three years, the Germans had murdered 93 percent of Lithuanian Jews, one of the highest victim rates in Europe. According to Yad Vashem, "By the time Germany surrendered to the Allies in 1945, only a few thousand Lithuanian Jews had survived" ("Lithuanian").*

My son and I were two of the few who survived in Lithuania.

---

*The exact percentage differs in different sources, but most reflect the 93%. In fact, some sources list an even higher percentage: 94%— 195,000 murdered out of 208,000 (answers.com); 90%—160,000 population that swelled to 250,000 with refugees (haaretz.com); 96%—based on 200,000 population (lithuanianjews.org.il); Largest percentage murdered based on 220,000 post-war population (jewish world. jpost.com—quoting Yad Vashem).

Mother's Voice
Chapter 4

For my family, the destruction of Druysk began with the Nazi invasion of the U.S.S.R. on June 22, 1941. Druysk was one of the villages in the Germans' path. Life was totally changed.

The *Holocaust Encyclopedia* article, "Invasion of the Soviet Union," details the history:

> Under the code name Operation Barbarossa, Nazi Germany invaded the Soviet Union on June 22, 1941, in the largest German military operation of World War II.
>
> The destruction of the Soviet Union by military force, the permanent elimination of the perceived Communist threat to Germany, and the seizure of prime land within Soviet borders for long-term German settlement had been a core policy of the Nazi movement since the 1920s. Adolf Hitler had always regarded the German-Soviet Non-Aggression pact, signed on August 23, 1939, as a temporary tactical maneuver. In July 1940, just weeks after the German conquest of France and the Low Countries, Hitler decided to attack the Soviet Union within the following year. On December 18, 1940, he signed Directive 21 (code-named Operation Barbarossa), the first operational order for the invasion of the Soviet Union.

From the beginning of operational planning, German military and police authorities intended to wage a war of annihilation against the Communist state as well as the Jews of the Soviet Union, whom they characterized as forming the "racial basis" for the Soviet state. During the winter and spring months of 1941, officials of the Army High Command (*Oberkommando des Heeres*-OKH) and the Reich Security Main Office (*Reichssicherheitshauptamt*-RSHA) negotiated arrangements for the deployment of special units (*Einsatzgruppen*) of the Security Police and the Security Service (*Sicherheitsdienst*-SD) behind the front lines to physically annihilate Jews, Communists, and other persons deemed to be dangerous to the establishment of long-term German rule on Soviet territory.

With 134 Divisions at full fighting strength and 73 more divisions for deployment behind the front, German forces invaded the Soviet Union on June 22, 1941, less than two years after the German-Soviet Pact was signed. Three army groups, including more than three million German soldiers, supported by 650,000 troops from Germany's allies (Finland and Romania), and later augmented by units from Italy, Croatia, Slovakia, and Hungary, attacked the Soviet Union across a broad front, from the Baltic Sea in the north to the Black Sea in the south. For months, the Soviet leadership had refused to heed warnings from the Western Powers of the German troop buildup along its western border. Germany and its Axis partners thus achieved almost complete tactical surprise. Much of the existing Soviet air force was destroyed on the ground; the Soviet armies were initially overwhelmed. German units encircled millions of Soviet soldiers, who, cut off from supplies and reinforcements, had few options other than to surrender.

As the German army advanced deep into Soviet territory, SS and police units followed the troops. The first to arrive were the *Einsatzgruppen* of the Security Police and the SD, which the RSHA tasked with identifying and eliminating persons who might organize and implement resistance to the German occupation forces, identifying and concentrating groups of people who were "hostile" to German rule in the East, establishing intelligence networks, and securing key documentation and facilities.

Often known as mobile killing units, the *Einsatzgruppen* initiated mass-murder operations, primarily against Jewish males, officials of the Communist Party and State, and Soviet Roma (Gypsies), and, often with assistance from German Army personnel, established ghettos and other holding facilities to concentrate large numbers of Soviet Jews.

Beginning in late July, with the arrival of Himmler's representatives, the higher SS and police leaders, and significant reinforcement, the SS and police, supported by locally recruited auxiliaries, began to physically annihilate entire Jewish communities in the Soviet Union. Success both on the military front and in the murder of the Soviet Jews contributed to Hitler's decision to deport German Jews to the occupied Soviet Union beginning on October 15, 1941, initiating what would become "Final Solution" policy: the physical annihilation of the European Jews. ("Soviet Union, Invasion of")

Druysk was one of those villages annihilated. After the area around Druysk was captured by the Germans in June of 1941, German law was established and anti-Jewish edicts were announced—the yellow star, exclusion from employment, and forced labor.

After the Germans attacked in 1941, Frumka Malka, with her daughters, made her way back to Vilna to join her husband.

In the winter of 1942, the Germans sent the Druysk Jews as well as those from Slabodka to the city of Vidzy about forty kilometers away. Jews from other *shtetls* were also sent to Vidzy, where a ghetto was established (Seligman).[14]

In Vidzy we were housed in overcrowded conditions not only in the synagogue and the *Beth Midrash* but also in houses in the ghetto area. In addition to the local population, Jews from Dubinovo, Druya, Druysk, Miory, Plussy, and Turmont were interned there. The population included both workers and the "non-productive," the old, the sick, and the frail.

The Jewish Genealogy site reports: "The first *Aktion* occurred [early in 1942]. Three thousand were killed. The local Lithuanian farmers actively helped the Germans" ("Druysk"). Lithuanians helped because the Germans had promised the Lithuanians that after the war they would have their own country and not be part of the USSR.

The local *Judenrat* (Jewish Council) organized work, "especially to cut peat from the bogs near Opsa and in various workshops" (Seligman). While we were in Vidzy, my husband and others in the family worked for the Nazis in the forests, cutting down trees to send back to Germany. Women sewed uniforms and mended uniforms for the German army; they also cooked and washed clothes for the Germans and the Lithuanians.

The ghetto was terrible. There was little food, so we were always hungry, and no wood to use for heat, so we were always cold. We sometimes could get food from the *Judenrat*, the government in the ghetto, or from the Jewish police. We couldn't go out of the ghetto except to work. A couple of young men and women, including me, went out to work. We worked for a priest. He was very generous to us; he gave us food (he didn't have to) and he paid us a little.

There was no social life in the ghetto—no music—nothing. We had always the same clothes. Nothing new! There was no place to bathe. Several people escaped and went to the partisans in the forests. People with children could not escape the ghetto. The partisans did not want any children whose cries could endanger the group.

We were in the Vidzy Ghetto for about three months. Then I heard rumors that they would be taking us to Swieciany (Polish), or Svencionys (Lithuanian) to another ghetto. I had a bad feeling about this.

My whole family, including my husband, Yosel, our son, Chaim, and me, were transferred to a small ghetto in Swieciany, where we were crowded into local community buildings together with Jews from twenty other communities (Seligman). The lack of food and poor sanitary conditions led to an outbreak
of typhus during which many died. We were in the Swieciany Ghetto for another three months, doing the same work as we had done in Vidzy Ghetto. (See Note 14.)

In March 1942, SS-*Sturmbannfuhrer* Horst Wulff, the Nazi *Gebeitskommissar* of the Vilna Province, decided to clear all the remaining ghettos in the border lands, ostensibly because of the rise in partisan activity in the area (Seligman). The number of partisans had increased because of escapees from the ghettos. The head of the Vilna *Judenrat*, Jacob Gens, was brought to Swieciany to inform us that those with useful professions were to be moved to Vilna, while the others were be transported to Kovno. That is when I begged my husband and family to escape.

Seligman writes, "Salek Dressler, the commander of the Vilna Jewish Police, arrived in the ghetto to arrange the transfer. Still panic spread through the community, for everybody understood from previous experience that it was essential to be among the group considered 'useful.' "

I had a strong premonition that the Nazis would kill us. I escaped from Swieciany Ghetto and went to my husband, sister, brother, brothers-in-law, sisters-in-law, and my nephews and nieces. I told them: "Let us go and hide ourselves. They will kill us all." They didn't believe me. I begged them to leave with me.

My husband and I were staying with a Christian family who let us sleep in their house. My husband worked for them, and I crocheted. He was told that they were looking for him. He said, "I am going."

I said to him, "Why are you going? Stay with me. We have a small child."

He said, "If I don't go, they will come for you. If you need us, come after us."

This is the last time I saw my husband and the rest of my family. They were taken to Ponar, where they were murdered.[15] I hid in a closet with Chaim for three days and then I fled to the forests with my son.

In April 1942, around Passover, the Jews from the ghetto "gathered at the station in Nowo-Swieciany and boarded the freight wagons under the guard of the Vilna Jewish Police" (Seligman).

Mother's Voice
Chapter 5

I *know exactly what happened to my husband and family because as they were taken on carts to Ponar, one of my cousins, Zalman Baron, was able to escape. After the war when he met us, he told us everything that had happened.*

The Gestapo and Lithuanian police took control of the train, detouring from Kovno to Ponar, the mass murder site. In 1940 and 1941, the Soviets dug six pits at Ponar for fuel storage tanks; however, the Soviets retreated before they could finish the project. The Germans, who occupied Lithuania after the Soviets, used the pits in the process of murdering Jews from Vilna and the outskirts. Between 1941 and 1944, "70,000 to 100,000 people," mostly Jews, were murdered at Ponar. ("Ponar").

Some, including my family, were taken on horse carts. When they arrived at Ponar, instead of at Vilna, they realized that they had been tricked and tried to escape. Six hundred Jews of Swieciany, Vidzy, Druysk, and Slobodka were murdered; bodies were strewn over the depot at Ponar and in the fields. Germans as well as Lithuanian *ypatingi buriai* (special forces; Lithuanian volunteers) were shot in the chaos. Most of the Jews were recaptured, brought to the pits, and murdered, shot by the Lithuanian police, the Security Police (Sipo) under Martin Weiss's command, and the *ypatingi buriai* (Seligman). There were six pits, two where the bodies were slain and left overnight and then taken the next day on gurneys to the third, fourth, and fifth pits to be burned. The sixth pit is where the workers lived. The sixth pit was the deepest; the workers had to climb a ladder to leave the pit. Each night the ladder was pulled up so that the workers could not escape (Sakowicz 123).

On April 6, Weiss ordered Jewish policemen from Vilna to accompany him to Ponar "to collect" the dead from the "woods and fields" and bury the bodies in the pits (Seligman).

A Jewish policeman at the trial of Martin Weiss described the scene as follows:

> When we left the Vilna Ghetto, we believed that we were parting from it forever. . . . Just before Ponar, the car stopped, and we were ordered to continue on foot. We could see peasants hurrying to their homes, bent with loads on their backs. They had profited from the belongings of the murdered. When we entered deeper into the woods, a horrifying spectacle was revealed to our eyes. The whole area was strewn with bodies and human limbs. Weiss took us to an enormous pit full of corpses and told us to cover them with earth. One policeman stopped and said *Kaddish*. After we had completely covered the bodies, Weiss led us to a second grave that he ordered us to cover. At the end of all this, he took us on a tour of the whole area and gave us explanations as though he were a guide at an exhibition: "Here are the graves of Jews kidnapped by abductors in 1941. Here is a second grave, that of the Provocation *Aktionen*." He then went on to the graves of the Vilna Ghetto's Yellow and Pink *Aktionen*. He indicated a grave in which priests were buried and other graves of Russian prisoners of war. At the conclusion of the tour, he ordered us to gather the bodies scattered over the area and throw them into a pit. (Seligman)

Mother's Voice
Chapter 6

After my husband and family were murdered, my son and I hid for a short while in the forest and then stayed for three months with the family for whom I was working and crocheting. The whole town knew we were there, but they never betrayed us; they didn't kill Jews. When the Germans came nearer, I realized it was becoming too dangerous for my son and me, so I left. I would still return to some of the Christian families there, however. They gave me food and something to take with me. Some people would let me bathe my son and myself on Saturday evenings.

I had to keep moving so the Germans would not realize I was in the area. I needed to change, not have a pattern. Sometimes people let me stay a little. One man warned me when the Germans came into town, telling me, "Go deep into the woods. The Germans are here." Then he gave me food and milk for my son. Usually I stayed in an area not too far from houses.

We were caught once. We were going to be shot in this pit. I was holding Chaim and I thought to myself: This is not the way that I am going to die! So with my son in my arms, I ran to the forest. A soldier shot but missed us. I think he missed us on purpose. Maybe he did not want to kill a woman with a child in her arms.

We hid in the forest in the daytime and walked only at night. I bent branches of bushes to make teepee style huts to hide or to lie in. I put leaves on the ground and covered my son and me with leaves. Occasionally we hid in haystacks.

Sometimes we hid in holes the farmers had dug to store their potatoes. If we were lucky, we found rotten potatoes, which tasted great to us.

There were other people in the forests: young men and women and Russian soldiers. People did not stay together; this was too risky. Sometimes I stayed with the children who took care of the cows and horses—cowherds. I would stay with them all day. They helped me sometimes. A Russian soldier, who had a three-year-old son at home whom he missed, would whistle, and my son, Chaim, would answer with a whistle. Sometimes people would take me to other places that were safe. I couldn't join the partisans because they did not want women with children. They had to move quickly at times and they were afraid children would slow them down. Moreover, the sound of a baby's or a toddler's cry could be fatal. A cry could give away the partisans' location to the Germans or Lithuanians, and then the group would be murdered. Although they did not want us in their *Otrads* (partisan unit), they occasionally gave us bread.

Later I heard from my stepdaughters about children where they were hidden. During two incidents, children started to cry and they were suffocated. This was a terrible dilemma for their parents: let the child cry and the whole group could be discovered and killed or kill the child to save the group. This was a "choiceless choice."

In 1943, the Germans killed a family for helping Jews. After this, I was not able to stay any place. People were scared to let me hide in their homes. Therefore, we stayed in the woods.

If I should believe in G-d, I would say G-d helped me. Also my son was a good boy. He never cried. I often carried my son on my shoulders. I told him, "Don't fall asleep." If he fell asleep, he fell backwards and then was very difficult for me to carry. But he was tired, so at times he did fall asleep.

Two weeks after the war had ended, I was still hiding. A Russian woman soldier saw me and said, "Why are you sitting there?" She told me the war was over. I had thought my son and I were the only ones left.

Later I learned about the Battle of Stalingrad and the Russian offensive. By the summer of 1944, Belarus was completely liberated. The *Holocaust Encyclopedia* confirms this:

> Despite catastrophic losses in the first six weeks of [Operation Barbarossa], the Soviet Union failed to collapse as anticipated by the Nazi leadership and the German military commanders. . . . . Nevertheless, by late September 1941, German forces reached the gates of Leningrad in the north.
>
> . . . . German units reached the outskirts of Moscow in early December. . . . . On December 6, 1941, the Soviet Union launched a major counterattack against the center of the front, driving the Germans back from Moscow in chaos. . . . . In the summer of 1942, Germany resumed the offensive with a massive attack to the south and southeast toward the city of Stalingrad (Volgograd) on the Volga River and toward the oil fields of the Caucasus. As the Germans reached the outskirts of Stalingrad and approached Groznyj (Groznyy) in the Caucasus, approximately 120 miles from the shores of the Caspian Sea in September 1942, the German domination of Europe reached its furthest geographical extension. ("Soviet Union, Invasion of")
>
> The battle for the city of Stalingrad proved a decisive psychological turning point, ending a string of German victories in the summer of 1942 and beginning the long retreat

westward that would end with Nazi Germany's surrender in May 1945.

In mid-November 1942, the Soviet army launched a massive counteroffensive against the German Sixth Army, some 250,000 soldiers trying to conquer Stalingrad in bitter hand-to-hand fighting. The Soviet troops encircled and trapped the German forces. Following six more weeks of fierce combat in which both sides took heavy casualties, some 91,000 surviving German soldiers surrendered between January 31 and February 2, 1943.

After the victory at Stalingrad, the Soviet army remained on the offensive, liberating most of the Ukraine, and virtually all of Russia and eastern Belorussia during 1943.

. . . . In the summer of 1944, the Soviets launched another major offensive, which liberated the rest of Belorussia and the Ukraine, most of the Baltic States, and eastern Poland from Nazi rule. ("Soviet Union and the Eastern Front")

I began to walk back to Druysk to see if anyone else was alive. On my way I met a tailor, who told me to go to his uncle's home because his uncle was Jewish and would surely help us.

He said, "Tell him I said to let you into his house."

I went to the uncle's house. He said, "you are not the first Jew to ask me for help."

I said to him, "I have bread. I don't ask for anything for myself but for my son. Give him a little."

He gave us nothing, even for the child. Chaim, who was four and a half then and didn't like to sleep inside, said, "Mom, let's go outside and cover ourselves with branches."

After the war, I saw the man in Germany. He talked with my second husband, Michel, in the *shul*. The man asked me to forgive him.

I continued my journey, going from one place to another closer to my hometown. When I came there, I looked for my husband and family. I looked for my sister. I found no one. I never again saw the Jews I had left in Swieciany. While in Druysk, I handled a little (bought and sold). I stayed in a house with twenty-one other survivors (eighteen adults and three children), including Michel Cypuk and his two daughters, who had been my neighbors before the deportations. His wife was dead. My husband was dead. He needed a mother for his two daughters, and I needed a father for my son.

Michel and another man did business together. One night I waited until my son was asleep because I needed to go with the man to do business. My son was so emotionally attached to me that he did not want to be separated from me. I went with this other man, who had hid himself in a barn during the war. We were on a horse and wagon when we were attacked by local people—Lithuanian Christians. I managed to escape, but he was killed. Lots of Lithuanians were afraid that Jews would identify them to the Soviets as collaborators with the Germans. The Soviets too were brutal. They would shoot former collaborators or send them to Siberia.

After this, we moved to another place. Michel and I married in 1945 in Braslav (Pol. Brasław), a small town in Belarus.[16]

Chapter 7-11 Son's Voice

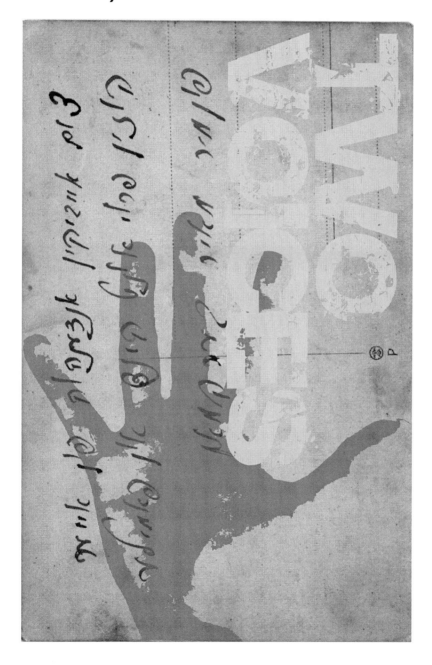

Son's Voice
Chapter 7

1941 had no Halley's Comet, but nonetheless it was a monumental year, a year of great destruction, a year of terrible losses. 1941 was the year of Operation Barbarossa when the Germans, in violation of the Non-Aggression Pact, turned on the Soviets on June 22, 1941, opening the Eastern Front (see note 9). The Nazis unleashed 4.5 million troops, attacking the Soviet Union along an 1800 mile front, laying waste their lands and killing helpless citizens. In 1941 as the *Wehrmacht* raped and plundered its way across the USSR, the *Einsatzgruppen* (special mobile killing units) followed, murdering thousands and thousands of Jews, living in *shtetls* and cities, for example at the Babi Yar massacre in the Ukraine.[17]

Later in 1941, on December 7, without a declaration of war, the United States Naval Base at Pearl Harbor on the island of O'ahu, Hawaii, was attacked by the Japanese. The Pearl Harbor Raid Overview reports: "Within a short time five of eight battleships at Pearl Harbor were sunk or sinking, with the rest damaged. Several other ships and most Hawaii-based combat planes were also knocked out, and over 2400 Americans were dead. Soon after, Japanese planes eliminated much of the American air force in the Philippines, and a Japanese army was ashore in Malaya." ("Pearl Harbor")

1941 was also the year I was born—January 25, 1941. I don't remember very much from my early years. I was born in Druysk, a *shtetl* that my mother has told me about. Druysk was an unusual town because the population consisted of Jews—523; Christians—0. There had never been a pogrom in Druysk.

My father, Yosel Berkman, was a cobbler, just the soles.[18] The customer brought the upper parts of the shoe, and my father attached the uppers to the soles or he repaired the soles on shoes. Yosel had a brother and sister. His father had died young. His mother, Shana, lived with us.

My mother, Sara, did handling—she sold salt, herring, needles, thread, and kerosene and went outside the village and sold these. My parents lived in a one room house with a thatched roof, a dirt floor, an outhouse, and a well for water right outside the house. My mother told me that the Soviets came in after the partition of Poland in 1939. They were Communists, but we were not. We were bourgeoisie. They rationed food and other commodities. People did not like them. People who owned land were taken to Siberia. We were not landowners, so they did not bother us. In fact, my mother worked in a Soviet store; they made her work there. She only sold three things in the Soviet store: herring, butter, and kerosene.

The Germans came in soon after I was born in 1941. My mother later told me that one day, when I was six months old, there were rumors of a German *Aktion* (operation involving the mass assembly, deportation, and murder of Jews). Everyone ran. However, my mother was not in the room, so my aunt who had four children, grabbed me and ran, leaving her own six-month-old baby on the bed. The rumor was a false one. When my mother returned, she asked her sister why she hadn't taken her own baby. My aunt answered: "You have only one child. I had to save him."

In 1942 the townspeople were removed from Druysk to a ghetto—a small ghetto in Vidzy, where my father and other male relatives cut peat and chopped down trees to be sent back to Germany (see note 14). The women stayed inside the ghetto—cooking for the men and children. Some worked for the Germans sewing and mending uniforms.

After several months they moved us to Swieciany Ghetto, a bigger ghetto (see note 14). There too the men worked in the woods cutting trees. When they were finished cutting the trees in one location, they were sent to the next forest. They had to be able to work or they were shot.

Then these workers, including my father and all my other relatives, were to be taken to a ghetto nearer to Vilna. Many were transported there from Vilna as well as from the small towns in the *Vilna Gubneria*. My mother had a premonition—very bad feelings—about this transport. She hid with me in a closet for three days. When all was quiet again and the commotion had died down, she came out of the hiding place.

From the ghetto near Vilna, my father, his mother, Shana, only fifty-two years old, our relatives, and the rest of the Jews from Druysk were taken to Ponar (Ponary) where there were killing pits. There they were murdered, burned, and buried.

I am haunted to this day, wondering if my father had to watch his mother murdered. I am glad he did not have to see my mother and me killed.

The six pits there had been used by the Russians for the storage of ammunition, kerosene, and gasoline. However, the Germans used two of these pits for killing men, women, children, and babies. Most of the killing was done by Lithuanians, supported by the Germans. In three other pits, the *Sonderkommandos* burned the bodies.[19] The *Sonderkommandos* lived in the sixth pit. The Lithuanians helped because they were grateful to the Germans for expelling the Soviets from Lithuania and promising the Lithuanians their freedom and, after the war, an independent Lithuania.

All the killing of the citizens of Druysk was done in three days in 1942. From the hundreds of Druysk Jews, only twenty -one people survived, including my stepsisters and me—eighteen adults and three children. Of forty-nine members of my family, including first cousins, only my mother and I survived.

After we had escaped deportation to Ponar, I remember we stayed for about three months in a monastery. The priest we knew arranged for us to hide there. The monks kept us for a while. My mother was kept there as a cleaning woman. They gave me a Polish name, Michas. One of the monks made a little cross for me. I walked around the monastery wearing this tiny cross. The monk also taught me Catholic prayers. When the Germans came around, the monks turned us away because they were afraid of being killed.

We then went into the woods, roaming the woods around Vilna until the end of the war. We went around searching for households that were sympathetic to Jews, for people who would give us bread. Basically we lived in the woods for almost three years, scrounging around for food.

My mother was good at healing, using plants from the woods. Once I had a bad infection on my head. During the night she went into a barn and got pitch that was used on the cart wheels, and she put that pitch on my head. Pitch is loaded with coal tar, the same ingredient that is in tar soap[20] and the black salve[21] that people used to use. The wound on my head healed. Another time my hands were covered with an infection. My mother took my urine and put this on my hands and they healed. Urine contains urea so perhaps this healed my infected hands. [22] Another time I had worms that came out in my stool. My mother saw this and fed me garlic, which helped.[23]

At the beginning we tried to hook up with the partisans; however, the partisans would not take my mother because she had a child. The partisans were afraid of children. They thought the children crying, if they were with the group, would disclose their hiding place. They would have taken her if she would leave me because she was handy and strong. But she did not want to leave me—thankfully! Therefore, the partisans would not take us. They chased us away. They were afraid that I would cry. Many people had suffocated their children rather than allowing them to cry and betray the group to the enemy.

Son's Voice
Chapter 8

I remember the cold in the forest. I was always cold. Neither mother nor I had warm clothing. I did not even have a jacket. Lithuania has very cold winters and where we were was particularly cold. I was always cold, cold!

Clothes were definitely a problem. I grew out of mine. Mother's clothing became tattered and worn. Throughout the war she had only one dress. By the end of the war there was no material available, not for anyone. Mother eventually had to carry me in the front of her body. I helped cover her, and also her body heat kept me warm.

To keep warm at night when we slept, my mother would make a shelter of branches, or she would look for potato pits.Poor people, at that time and place, didn't have basements, so they dug holes in the ground where it was colder but where it would not freeze. They stored their extra food such as potatoes in these holes. They would line the holes with leaves, drop the potatoes in, and then cover the opening with a board, and place more leaves on top of the board. Potatoes were very important because they were one of the staples; peasants ate bread, potatoes, and herring.

My mother found these holes by scuffing her shoes along the ground. When she found a pit, we would sleep there. We would crawl in, piling leaves on top of us to keep warm. At night, in these holes we were warmer than we would have been, exposed to the wind, snow, and cold.

We awoke early in the morning. First thing: we would try to find water. The morning dew settled on leaves, so we licked the leaves or the blades of grass.

Then mother and I foraged for berries, wild mushrooms, anything that grew in the forest or fields. We often went in to fields to steal a little corn. Corn from the fields was the best—sweet.

Toward the end of the war we found a dead horse. Mother cut pieces from the carcass and we ate them. We ate them raw; we could not have a fire because it would have signaled the Nazis that we were in the woods. In addition, mother had no way to light a fire. I still remember the good taste of meat.

After we ate something, we would hide in the forest for the rest of the day; we could not risk being seen. Mother would make a shelter of branches where we could rest until nightfall.

At night we looked for more food. Then we could go up to houses; this was too dangerous during the day. We looked through the windows to see if inside there was a woman alone. Women tended to be more sympathetic. If a woman was in the house alone, my mother would knock. However, my mother would try not to knock if through the window she saw a man. But sometimes we were so hungry, she had to knock anyhow. She was afraid a man would turn us in. Some women and some men helped. Most turned us away.

After we ate, we looked for a place to sleep during that night.

This is how we spent most of our days and nights while we were hiding in the forests.

Son's Voice
Chapter 9

*F*or approximately a year during the last part of the war, we stayed with a poor Polish grandmother—a *Babcia*, an old grandmother. She was an old beggar woman whom we knew. Her small barn housed a pig downstairs, and we lived in the little loft above. If Babcia had extra food, she would throw us a piece. But my mother still scrounged around for food.

Babcia was very religious and she thought she was saving our souls. She thought that saving us would give her the graces to help her to get to heaven when she died. She had a sister who apparently had a mental problem because Babcia told me (I spoke Polish and White Russian by this time), "Don't let my sister see you because she will give you away."

If Babcia's sister was not at home, she let us down from the loft and brought us into the house. Babcia's hut was very small with a sand and dirt floor.

Babcia had a brick or clay oven, a *Pripetchik*, in which she cooked and kept food, such as bread, warm.[24] In the lower half were the flames; in the top a space to warm food. I fit into this space and sometimes lay there and was warm and toasty.

I could crawl into the space in the oven. Mother couldn't. Under her bed, Babcia had a potato hole, the kind the peasants made in the woods, but this one was under Babcia's bed. Mother could not stand in there because she was about 5' 3". I could stand up in the potato hole. If we heard the Germans around, she got us down into the hole. This was safer than being in the loft of the barn.

During the day we slept, crawling inside the warm hay that lined the loft. We didn't dare go out during daylight. To keep me occupied my mother taught me how to knit. She gave me sticks to use as needles. I don't know for sure where she got the yarn. I do remember her unraveling a little thread from the bottom of her deteriorating dress. I would knit three rows and then she would unravel my knitting.

After the war, when the Soviet convoys came by, I would sit by the road and knit and they would throw us food.

At night we would go out. I hated to go out in the wintertime and search for food. At times we ate grass. I remember that I was always hungry.

Son's Voice
Chapter 10

During this time I was like a little wild animal. I didn't like to sleep indoors. I was very attached to my mother. I had to be with her at all times; we were inseparable. I didn't realize what was happening. Once in a while we heard shooting. I remember a bomb. In fact, I am deaf in one ear, which my mother thinks is from a bomb that went off near me.

My mother said that I was very quiet and basically this is what saved us. She said that I never cried.

Sometimes we ran across some partisans or a couple people fleeing. We tried to stay away from the non-Jewish partisans, for if they had known we were Jews, they would have killed us.

One night we ran across a Jewish man who was going to a farmer to get some food. My mother had a little metal jar that she carried with her in case she was able to get milk for me. This man said, "I'll take your jar and get some milk from the farmer." Later we found him dead with the jar near his body. This has always bothered me. When my mother saw his lifeless body, she grabbed my hand and ran.

Mother always talked about this kind man. She felt guilty because she thought that he may have died trying to help us.

Son's Voice
Chapter 11

When the Soviet front arrived in Lithuania, in July 1944, in the area where we were hiding, the war was over for us. However, for two weeks afterwards, we did not know that war was over. Looking through slits between the wallboards in the barn, we saw activity; we had seen German soldiers running. We also saw Soviet soldiers. We were again afraid. The Soviets were not always sympathetic.

We stayed in the loft until we saw many Soviet soldiers coming. My mother decided to take a chance. She told this Russian soldier we encountered who we were. He was outraged that a woman and child were living in the woods. He thought it was terrible that no one had taken us in and cared for us.

Mother decided to walk back towards Druysk. At this time we were near Vilna—50 or 60 kilometers away. My mother was afraid to be picked up by a Soviet convoy. She carried me in front. We walked at night. On the street when I would knit, the soldiers threw me salami. It was like a game; they thought I was cute. One of them gave my mother a jacket. Finally one soldier, a Russian Jew, took a liking to us and drove us to Druysk.

In order to obtain food, mother had to beg. She always took me, carrying me on her shoulder. If I fell asleep, I would be facing her back and falling back, which was a strain on her back and shoulders.

Moreover, I was growing and heavier. Mother always took me with her because there was no place to leave me when she went around begging for food or milk.

When we reached our hometown, nineteen others had also returned. A total of twenty-one of the five hundred and twenty-three! And one of the twenty-one was killed *after* the war was over!

Our house had been disassembled and carried away by non-Jews from the area because the house had been recently constructed and, thus, the timbers were relatively new. There was nothing on our lot.

When the town was evacuated, any peasant who wanted a house took it. The Lithuanian peasants were sympathetic to the Germans because the Germans gave them back their country, and they were no longer under the Soviets. Every house, but one, was occupied by a farmer. Only my uncle's house was empty. The twenty-one survivors, *She'arit Hapleta* (the surviving remnant) stayed there, hoping others would return.

Sarah Tsipa, the daughter of our neighbor Michel (she later became my sister), was sent to friends in Braslav, a nearby town. She went there to study at the gymnasium because she was older and the gymnasium near us had been eliminated. Sarah Tsipa only studied there for a several weeks.

Zelda went to the local school in Druysk. Because of the shortage of paper, students were writing on the backs of photographs. Zelda looked at these and saw that they were our photographs, and she brought home the photographs that she recognized.

My mother began to barter again, for example, kerosene for eggs. One night when I was sleeping, she went on a horse-drawn cart with this man she knew in order to do business nearby. Along the way, Lithuanian partisans, who had sided with the Germans, attacked the cart. The man was shot and killed by the Lithuanians. My mother jumped off the cart and ran into the woods. The partisans didn't chase her. She then decided that Druysk was no longer a place where we could safely live.

One of the Jews who returned was our former neighbor, Michel Cypuk. Michel, an uppers shoemaker with a little leather tanning factory, had lived across the street with his wife and two daughters, Sarah Tsipa and Zelda. He had survived the war in hiding. He had gold coins with which he paid off a Lithuanian non-Jew, Mr. Ctoska, who saved eighteen Jews in his home—in the basement and in shacks on his property. Tragically there was not enough food for everyone. Michel's wife died of starvation in her daughter Sarah's arms. So he had no wife and needed a mother for his daughters, and my mother had no husband and needed a father for her son. Their marriage was a marriage of convenience. My mother knew by this time that my father was dead. After the group was shot at Ponar, one wounded man survived among the dead and crawled out of the pit at night. The Lithuanians were so drunk that they did not see him. He then ran away. After the war when he encountered us, he told us what had happened. We had always hoped that my father was still alive. The man's story confirmed our fears.

We stayed only a couple of months in Druysk. I was either five and a half or six years old. We then all went to Braslav, a small town seven miles from Druysk. None of the remaining nineteen survivors stayed in Druysk. We hoped to hear news of our loved ones or to find them. We hooked up with more people; we were then about thirty people. The Russians told us that the Polish could go back to Poland. We had no identity papers; they had been destroyed; however, because my mother spoke excellent Polish, she convinced them that we were Polish. Therefore, they allowed us to return to Poland.

However, before we left Braslav, Lithuania, for Poland, we went by train to Ponar. We went to the pits where we saw ashes. For the rest of her life, my mother remembered the stench that came from the pits. My mother said *Kaddish* (a prayer recited by mourners) for my father, her sisters and brothers, and the rest of our relatives.[25] We also went to find Frumka Malka's grave in the woods outside Vilna. She and her daughters had been murdered by a school friend and buried. He had been forced to tell where she was buried. Michel went with us, and we found the grave with no marker. Michel found an old table in the woods and dragged it on top of the grave as a marker. My mother said *Kaddish*. We don't know what happened to Frumka Malka's husband.

This was my mother's sad goodbye to her beloved family. We continue to commemorate their deaths on the first day of *Nissan*, the month of redemption, around Passover, when we say *Kaddish*.

After Ponar we returned to Braslav and then left with the rest of the group for Warsaw, Poland. Because there were no trains to Warsaw at this time, we bribed a Russian army driver to take us to Poland. We sat in the back of his truck. When we arrived in Warsaw, we thought we would be safe.

Warsaw is the capital and a huge city. We did not expect to encounter antisemitism there. However, on our way to synagogue we were beaten up. Then we really wanted to leave Poland. We heard that if we could get to Germany we could go to the American zone. Therefore, we decided to escape to the Allied camps in Germany. Moreover, my mother did not want to be under Communist rule. The first time we tried to cross the border we were caught and put in jail for six weeks.

When we got out of jail, we were determained to cross the border to reach Germany. However, we needed money for bribes. Michel had twelve gold coins from Russian imperial times of Czar Nicholai II;

five rouble coins were issued during his reign 1897-1911. If Michel had been caught with these gold coins, he would have been shot. Therefore, my mother covered the coins with material, making buttons of seven of them. She sewed the seven buttons onto my jacket—five down the front and one on each sleeve. She made soap and put two coins inside the soap. The other three she put into candy she had made from caramelized sugar. We still have two gold coins left.

About this time, the group of thirty survivors split up into smaller groups. Our group totaled eleven. We bribed Russian postal workers with ten gold coins. They put us in sacks, like mail, and placed us in two trucks that were going to East Berlin to deliver mail and other supplies to the Russians. So that is how we were smuggled into East Berlin, part of the Soviet Zone, which was in chaos. The Russians were taking their revenge on the Germans so they weren't worried about us. From East Berlin, we escaped to West Berlin, part of the American Zone, which was under the control of U.S. soldiers.It was easy to go from East to West Berlin then. We stayed in a West Berlin Displaced Persons (DP) Camp for a couple of months.[26] This DP camp was under American control. I was sent to a school there, but I was like a wild animal and did not want to be away from my mother; therefore, I would run away every day.

We then went to another camp that was American controlled— Ziegenhain Displaced Persons Camp in the Frankfurt district.[27] Here too we tried to find relatives. We were given cigarettes and stockings as part of our rations. We could trade stockings for anything. We were also given bananas and peanut butter, which we had never seen before. The bananas tasted awful. Nobody had told us to peel them. The peanut butter looked like brown stuff and smelled funny— unappetizing. We threw the peanut butter out. They gave us bubble gum too. They meant well. However, we had never seen this before.

We fell asleep with the bubble gum in our mouths and it ended up in our hair. What a mess!

After three months in Ziegenhain DP Camp, we went to Eschwege DP Camp, also in the American Zone, where we stayed for over three years.[28] A *Holocaust Encyclopedia* article explains, "Eschwege, a former German air force base in the Frankfurt district of the American-occupied zone, became a DP camp in January 1946" ("Eschwege"). Eschwege was also a prison camp for Polish prisoners with barbed wire and guard posts and American Military police (MPs). The DPs numbered about 3,500. The camp was run by United Nations Relief and Rehabilitation Administration (UNRRA).[29] We, however, had our own government and guards. My stepfather had to guard once in a while. The buildings were dormitory-type buildings with one main bathhouse, only showers, no bathtubs. We established a *mikvah*.[30] On Friday nights we took baths.

> Eschwege housed approximately 1,770 Jews at the time of its opening and its young population quickly developed a revitalized community, evidenced by the opening of a kindergarten with 50 children by April 1947. [Don says this was an elementary school and not for children his age.] Eschwege also had a *Talmud Torah*, a *cheder*, and a *yeshiva*, as well as a *Bet Ya'akov* religious high school for girls.
>
> Religious life was also celebrated in the camp's several synagogues and a mikvah. Eschwege had a sports club with 100 players, a movie theater, a 500-seat auditorium, and a theater group. The camp published the newspaper *Undzer Hofenung* (Our Hope).
>
> At its peak, on October 19, 1946, Eschwege housed roughly 3,355 Jews. The camp closed on April 26, 1949. ("Eschwege")

A *Betar*-affiliated group in Eschwege DP Camp prepared even the young for self-defense—to go to Palestine to fight.[31] Zelda and I were given uniforms with the insignia of *Betar* (a menorah) and little wooden guns. They marched us, which was fun for kids, similar to cowboys and Indians. They were constantly training us. There were only a few children my age in the whole camp, maybe about a dozen. Most survivors were young people of fighting age. (See Photographs section.)

I began to know my stepfather better. He had lost all his family except for his two daughters. The older daughter, Sarah Tsipa, was sixteen years old. In 1947, she went to another DP camp to study. My stepfather, Michel, was afraid that she would go into the Israeli Defense Force. Although they had come to talk to us about going to Palestine, he felt that he had lost enough family; he didn't want to lose Sarah. Therefore, he was afraid to go to Palestine. Michel wanted to immigrate to Australia, Argentine, Canada, or the United States.

His first choice was Australia. After the *Shoah*, "proportional to population size, only Israel accepted more Holocaust survivors than Australia." By 1961, "35,000 pre-war Jewish refugees and post-war Holocaust survivors had immigrated to Australia." Today there are Holocaust Centers in Sydney and Melbourne ("Rebuilding Jewish Lives").

The reason the U.S. was his last choice was that Michel's uncle, a cantor, who had gone earlier to visit the U.S. with an eye to settling there, didn't like the country; he said that it was not religious enough.

The more I knew my stepfather, the more I liked him. I never knew my real father, Yosel; Michel was my father. Sisters were sisters. We got along some days and others, not. When my older stepsister, Sarah, was eighteen, she moved to another camp. There she met and married David. I was closer to my other sister, Zelda; we lived in the same camp and grew up together. As adults the three of us have a wonderful, loving relationship—we have a strong bond.

They are my dear sisters!

We had the basics in the camp. We had bread we made from flour the Red Cross gave us.[32] They gave us school supplies: rulers, paper, pens, and pencils. Different organizations provided some of the equipment for these schools.

The older kids had school with teachers who had survived. We younger ones didn't have regular school, but we had a *cheder* (Hebrew school). An older man who knew Hebrew script and the Torah taught us during regular school hours but did not teach us regular school subjects, such as math.

We were trying to get back to normal. I was wild. They had a problem with me. I didn't like to be inside houses; I wanted to be outside. I didn't like to sit in school. I suppose this is understandable when I consider that I was brought up in the woods. In school if I made a noise, the teacher hit me with a ruler. If I didn't answer, he hit me with a whip. I ran away several times. I didn't have far to run.

We were on our own after school. I played soccer with the other kids. A U.S. soldier had given us a soccer ball that we kicked around. We didn't need toys; we improvised. The camp had one oven—"a little crematorium," so we played with the oven. We knew what a crematorium was because the older people in camp talked about that. They showed us where, they said, the body fat dripped down. They said the "Nazis made soap from this fat." [33] *In fact, when I was older, I wondered about this because Eschwege had been a German Air Force base not a concentration camp. Perhaps bread was baked in the oven.*

My mother was trying to make life better for us. People moonlighted by trading in diamonds. Mother began cleaning other refugees' rooms, for this she was given an orange or a banana.

I remember our approximately four years in the DP Camps as boring and hard. We were always hungry. We often had fights with each other because of boredom. We never had enough clothing. Rooms were small; children slept on the floor. The rooms were infested with mice and rats, which crawled over us at night. Altogether it was certainly better than the woods, it was not ideal for a young boy who should have been learning subjects other than Hebrew.

Chapter 12 Mother's Voice

Mother's Voice
Chapter 12

We were four survivors, Michel, Zelda, Chaim, and I, in Ziegenhain and Eschwege DP Camps. Sarah was in another camp. The camps were in the American Zone in Germany, supervised by UNRRA. We wanted to leave Europe—to emigrate from Germany. I wanted to go to Israel; however, my husband, Michel, was not healthy. If we went to Israel, we needed to be healthy and also to have some money. Also, Sarah, his older daughter was fighting age and he was afraid to lose her. He wanted first to go to Australia, then Argentina, third to Canada, and last choice, the United States.

The reason Michel was hesitant about the U.S. was that a cantor he knew had gone to the U.S. but had returned to Europe because, he said, the U.S. was not religious. This cantor was killed during the Holocaust.

Michel had a cousin, Mrs. Gordon, in the United States, in St. Paul, Minnesota, where they had a number of Jews. She found him through the Red Cross and sent papers to us. My son came as a Cypuk (Michel's last name; in the U.S. his last name became Chipkin, more English). As a Cypuk, Chaim would not need his own papers, which were difficult to obtain. Mrs. Gordan promised that she would provide work for us and gave us an affidavit that we would not become a burden on the government. Mrs. Gordon was poor; her husband was a taxi cab driver. She did a huge *mitzvah* for us. She and her husband were exceptionally kind to us. I still miss St. Paul, Minnesota; the people were very gracious and welcoming to us.

However, life in St Paul was very hard. We didn't know a word of English—not one word. Minnesota was very, very cold in the winter and 104° in the summer. I washed floors in houses. I also worked at home—doing hemming and other sewing. I earned a dollar an hour. We had a roomer who paid us three dollars a week, but I didn't like having a roomer. My daughter, Riva, was born in Minnesota. My husband worked very hard, but he had high blood pressure and bad kidneys.

My stepdaugther Sarah and her husband, David, came to the U.S. a half year later, settling in New York.

A friend who had a farm in South Jersey came to visit us. He told us that we could make a living more easily on a chicken farm. In 1954, we bought a farm in Oceanville, New Jersey, near Atlantic City. I suffered sixteen years on this farm—chicken and eggs! But I got along well with the chickens; they didn't speak English and neither did I. Still I worked long, long hours, from sunrise to sunset.

Many survivors had bought chicken farms, not in Oceanville but in Vineland, Mays Landing, and Egg Harbor. The American Jews were not interested in us. They said, "If you don't like America, go back." When we first came, they asked us what had happened as if they had never read a newspaper or heard the radio. This was at the beginning, but later things changed when they realized what we had experienced.

In 1970 we closed the farm. We could not make a living there. Egg prices had dropped and grain prices had skyrocketed. We then bought a house in Margate to be closer to my son and his family. Michel passed away in 1974.

My son was ambitious; at twenty-five years old, he bought a pharmacy in Brigantine. I worked with him there. He bought another

store in Brigantine—before he was thirty. Then he bought yet another
store in Absecon and later started a pharmacy in Linwood. He always
strove to succeed.

Chapter 13-15 Son's Voice

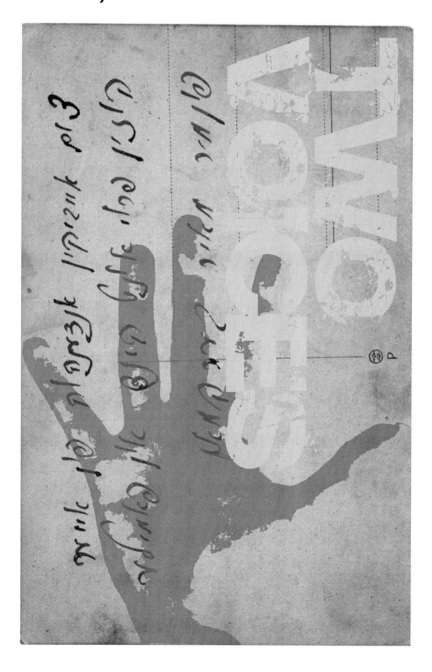

Son's Voice
Chapter 13

We knew we had to leave Eschwege DP Camp, which was scheduled to close in 1949. Many of the countries had quotas—Australia, Argentina, Canada, United States, and Palestine (*Eretz Israel*). In 1949, my stepfather's cousin in St. Paul, Minnesota—Mrs. Gordon—found us through the Red Cross and signed for us. She signed that the U.S. would not need to be responsible for us. This cousin was poor; her husband was a taxi cab driver. We were very excited to come to America. We were all happy, thinking that America grew trees with gold leaves.

We left Eschwege DP Camp on June 7, 1949, traveling to Bremen to catch a U.S. Navy destroyer to take us to America. We were aboard the boat for nine days; it took us that long to cross the Atlantic Ocean because the U. S. Navy was doing naval exercises. Everyone was seasick except for my stepfather and me. On the ship we used to watch the officers put their feet up on their desks. We had never seen people do this before; we found this funny and barbaric at the same time.

We arrived in New York Harbor on June 16, 1949, at 4 A.M.; every one started to shout: "The Statue of Liberty! There is the Statue of Liberty!" We ran to the upper deck to see Lady Liberty as we passed. We were deliriously happy. The *goldene medina*!

We docked at Ellis Island and were met by the Red Cross. We were disinfected and given donuts, which were so good that I over-ate, becoming nauseous and vomiting. We were also met by my stepfather's two uncles, who took us to a restaurant. For the first time I had watermelon and white bread. Again I ate so much that I became nauseated and vomited. My parents borrowed $50.00 from the uncles and then we boarded a train for St. Paul, Minnesota.

There were sixty of us who came through Ellis Island from that ship, yet we are not registered at Ellis Island, possibly because we came on a destroyer.

My mother, Michel, Zelda, and I traveled on to St. Paul, Minnesota, where we lived for five years, until 1954.

When we arrived in Minnesota, there was a lot of work to be done. Because we were so poor and my stepfather would not take handouts, my mother cleaned houses. My stepfather worked in a factory cutting leather. There were no other survivors working in the factory, so he was isolated. He also was very ill—heart, liver, kidneys, everything! I didn't know any English, so I worked in a junkyard taking old batteries out of junkers; I was eight or nine years old then. Zelda worked in a bakery. Because the bakery was not allowed to sell day-old baked goods, Zelda would bring home stale bread and donuts in the empty flour bags. I loved those jelly donuts.

My stepfather never wanted to take anything for nothing. I believe he had been influenced by the Musar Movement[34] that began in Lithuania and was founded by Rabbi Yisrael Salanter there in the mid nineteenth-century.[35] Rabbi Salanter was an ethical person as well as religious. Rabbi Salanter taught that if you borrowed anything, you pay it back as fast as you could. On the other hand, if you lent something, you do not ask for it but wait until the person gives the item back. Rabbi Salanter would not take anything from his government, so my stepfather would not take anything from the U. S. government. He felt that the U.S. had been good to him, allowing him to immigrate to the U.S. He was very happy the day he became a citizen.

I was nine years old and they put me in kindergarten. It was degrading, at nine, to be with five year olds, singing "Ring around the Rosie."

The first year I was skipped to the third grade and to another grade the following year. So I caught up quickly.

A friend from Oceanville, New Jersey, came to visit. He saw that my father was very ill. The friend had a chicken farm and wanted us to go in with him. He told my stepfather, "The fresh air in Oceanville will be better for you." We came to New Jersey in December of 1954 to a chicken farm on Leeds Point Road in Oceanville.[36] The house was built in the late 1800s. There were only five farmers in the area, but no children to play with. I amused myself building and setting animal traps. I was good at setting traps for wild dogs, possums, and owls that killed chickens when we let them outside their coops.

Life on a chicken farm is very difficult. There was no modern equipment on the farm or in the house. It was a hard life! We had outside plumbing pipes and those pipes froze in the winter. In the winter we went in a bucket which we carried outside and dumped in the cesspool.

One time my stepfather said, "We can't afford to have the cesspool pumped out. We have to build another cesspool next to the old one for the overflow." So I was the one to build this. I dug a hole six feet deep next to the old cesspool. Usually the next step would be to line the hole with bricks. We didn't do this. However, the overflow did go into the cesspool I built. Eventually this one caved in, but it had done its job.

There was no shower in the farmhouse, only a bathtub with claw feet. (I didn't take a shower until I went to college.) The water pressure was terrible. Water was precious. Once a week we drew a bath: first my sister, then me, next my mother, and last my stepfather—all in the same tub of water. In the summer so we would not run out of water for the chickens, we went to Lily Lake to bathe. We took soap and towels and bathed there.

Later my stepfather said that we would have done better if we had not gone on the farm. From the beginning nothing went right. We had bought 20,000 leghorn chickens to begin our egg farming. Most caught cholera and died. In the late 60s, egg prices dropped; therefore, they stopped farming.

My parents bought a home in Margate on Rumson Avenue in 1970. Sadly, my stepfather only lived in this house for four years before he passed away in November of 1974.

Son's Voice
Chapter 14

*I*n 1954, when we came to the farm, I was in the eighth grade. After the eighth grade, I went to Pleasantville High School. I was the only Jew in my class, so I had a lot of trouble because I was Jewish, even on the bus. Some of the children would torment me, singling me out, saying, "Here comes the Jew. Here comes the Jew." I had some fights in high school. Riva, who later went to Oakcrest, at that time the new high school, did not experience antisemitism.

When I was in high school, my mother went to the rabbi and asked him what my English name should be. He told her, "Donald." Donald is a Scottish name, meaning "world leader." A strong name.

In 1956, when I was in the tenth grade, I had a problem with my homeroom teacher, Mrs. H., who was also my science teacher. Every morning in homeroom the teacher made us read from the New Testament. I told her that I could not read from the New Testament but that I would read from the Old Testament, my Bible. She sent me to the principal because I refused to read. The principal was a good man, and after I explained to him the reason I refused to read, he told me he would discuss this with the teacher.

That night I heard a knock on the door. I opened the door to Mrs. H., whom I invited in.

She said, "Donald, I would like to speak with your parents."

I replied, "Mrs. H., my parents will understand nothing you say."

Mrs. H. said, "I would like to speak to them."

I called my mother and stepfather in. I interpreted for them what Mrs. H said, and I explained to her what my stepfather said: "He cannot read from the New Testament for religious reasons. Our Bible is the Old Testament. He can read from that."

Mrs H. never called on me again. I got an A in science.

During high school, in the summer, starting when I was fifteen, I worked at Al Rossman's Deli. He took a liking to me and was very good to me. I took the bus from Oceanville to Atlantic City at 9 AM, started working at 10 AM, worked until 8 PM, and then took the last bus to Oceanville at 9 PM.

In my senior year, in 1958, I was accepted at Georgia Tech for engineering and also at Long Island University Pharmacy School. I chose the university pharmacy school.

I enjoyed college even though I worked my way through. From 1958 to 1962, I lived with my sister Zelda and her husband, Danny. Zelda had gone to New York in 1952 to live with Sarah. She had met Danny there. In 1958, they had a two-bedroom apartment in Whitestone, New York, in Queens, and by then they had a child. They bought me a rolling bed that I folded up every morning.

Later, in 1959, they moved to Plainview, Long Island, to a four-bedroom home, and they gave me my own room for three years, until I graduated. I also ate with them. Sometimes I could give them some money for food, but not often. I would try to help as much as I could. They were very, very good to me. I will never forget their kindness.

I was going to go on to medical school, but there was no money and I was tired. I was only twenty-one and tired! I had worked after college until 10:00 PM and then went home to do homework. I went to bed around 1:00 AM, would get up at 7:00 AM, and then leave for college in Brooklyn.

By 1952, Germany had begun to discuss reparations. I never took reparations. I didn't want to take the money; I felt the German government was trying to buy me. My mother, stepfather, and Sarah took them. Zelda and I did not. I cannot be bought. I cannot accept money for the lives lost. I will not accept blood money. Giving it to charity is not an option for me. I will not accept anything from the German government—they cannot be absolved from their crimes with reparations.

Son's Voice
Chapter 15

I met my future wife, Nan Adler, in my junior year, on August 25, 1961. She went to Ithaca College and lived on Long Island. Nan and her parents were born in the U. S. Her grandparents were from Germany. We met on a blind date. I had been dared to take a date to see Harry Belafonte, a well-known American musician, at Forest Hills, New York.[37] Tickets were $25.00 each, which was a lot of money in those days. We married on August 26, 1962, a year and a day later. We have been together ever since—forty-seven years married as of 2009.

Nan is a speech therapist, and she taught in Vineland until our first son was born. We have three children, Joel born in 1964, Alan in 1967, and Michelle in 1968, and five grandchildren, Logan, Chloe, Lanie, Mason, and Sara (named after my mother). Joel, his wife, and children live nearby so they saw my mother often. Nan was good to my mother. She often took her shopping and other places and made sure she had whatever she needed.

Nan and I have made compromises about religion. Nan belonged to Reform Judaism.[38] I belonged to Orthodox Judaism that adheres to a relatively strict interpretation and application of the laws and ethics.

I'll never forget the first time I saw Nan eat a cheeseburger. This mix of meat and cheese was not kosher.[39] As an Orthodox Jew, I had never seen anyone do this![40] We compromised and met in Conservative Judaism (the term conservative signifies that Jews should attempt to conserve Jewish tradition and does not imply the movement's adherents are politically conservative).[41]

I have been successful in business. After graduating from pharmacy school in 1962, I worked in pharmacies in Brigantine and Absecon. In 1965, the owner of the Brigantine pharmacy wanted to sell, so I bought that pharmacy. I also had a pharmacy in Linwood but sold that to my business partner. I sold the Brigantine pharmacy in 1982. This was a good time to get out of the pharmacy business. At this time the prescription drug programs came in. We were filling more prescriptions than ever and making less money. I sold at a good price.

There were three pharmacies in Brigantine, mine and two others. So I bought one of those pharmacies in Brigantine in 1970, closed the pharmacy department, and opened a beach store. In Absecon, in 1984, I opened a large convenience store. The Absecon store was eventually taken over by the state under eminent domain to make a new road, which was never built.

I now have only the Brigantine store, which is open for seven months and closed for five months—it's a beach store. Nan helps me in Brigantine in the summer. Retail is rough. But during the time the store is closed, we are privileged to travel. Nan and I share a love for travel, and traveling gives me a respite because I am somewhat distracted when we are on a new adventure. However, when we are visiting poor rural areas, those memories come back!

I occasionally experience antisemitism in business. Through the years I have heard people make remarks about Jews when they aren't satisfied with something about my store. Why do they assume merchants are Jewish? How do they know that we are? This makes me angry.

Once I went to court. I caught a kid stealing, and I said to him, "You have something in your pocket belonging to us." I asked him to take the item out of his pocket.

His grandmother was there and cursed, "Dirty Jew. Jew bastard."

I took her by the hand, so I would not lose my temper, and walked her out. I was arrested for touching her, but the court threw the case out.

Chapter 16 Mother's Reflection

Mother's Reflection
Chapter 16

When we came to the United States, Chaim was almost nine years old and in public school. He was placed in kindergarten in public school because he did not yet know any English but eventually skipped grades as soon as he learned English. He sold papers, and I went with him to protect him. He also worked in a junk yard taking batteries out of cars. Then he went to college and had a pharmacy and beach store in Brigantine. He told his children about the Holocaust through a film; they sat together and watched a television series about the Holocaust (1978).

My son went back to Ponar, Latvia, and Druysk. He couldn't recognize anything. I am afraid to go back because I know what they did after the war. Then after I came here, I could not afford to go back.

Thank G-d I have my son, daughters, sons-in-law, daughter-in-law, and grandchildren. They are very nice to me, generous with their time and love.

*   *   *

When I worked in my son's store, this German man came in. He was twenty-three or twenty-four.

He asked me, "Do you forgive me?"

I said, "Never forgive. Never forget." No, it was not his fault, but who knows what his father or grandfather did?

Never forgive. Never forget. But still we need to be open with people.

Chapter 17 Son's Reflection

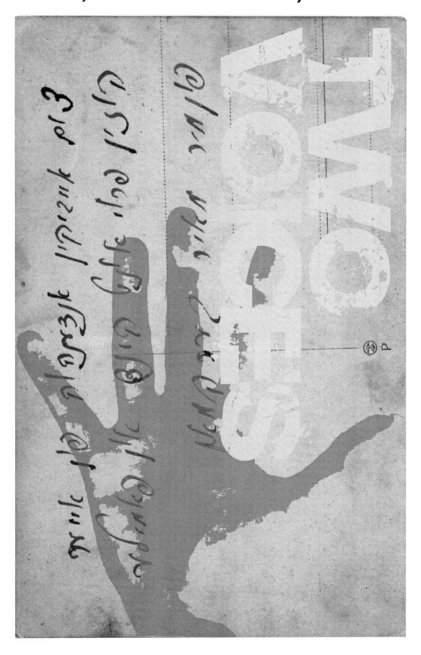

Son's Reflection
Chapter 17

I am bitter, still very bitter. I think: I was born at the wrong place, at the wrong time. Why me?

In Margate, few people my own age are child Holocaust survivors. There are second generation, but I am first generation. The ones born in the camps after the war are not considered survivors. I felt isolated.

Then I heard about a group for Child Survivors, those born between 1931 and 1945, called N.A.H.O.S., the National Association of Jewish Child Holocaust Survivors, Inc. and another group, founded by Ann Shore, president of the New York-based Hidden Child Foundation. From these organizations, I learned the importance of participating in groups with other Holocaust survivors. E. Fogelman and H. Bass-Wichelhaus explain the following:

> Holocaust child survivors profoundly benefit from participating in a variety of group modalities. From participant observation and interviews we demonstrate that affiliation in organizations, social events, commemorations, rituals, and in particular therapeutic groups each contributes to the well-being of Holocaust child survivors. Mourning is enhanced by joining forces with others from a historical event that left many children orphans, bereft of a home, a community, a country, and an identity. Group participants

achieve individuation and ego integration, and gain clarity
about the complex psychological consequences of surviving
the Holocaust. A fragmented identity is restored through the
opportunity of interacting with others whose identity has
been ruptured by similar cataclysmic events. (Abstract)

Groups like the Hidden Child Foundation are invaluable for hidden
children like me, but I still have nightmares and feel guilty.

I had reoccurring dreams in the camp, but when I came to the
U. S., these stopped. They started up again in 1992 when my first
grandchild was born.

I feel guilty that I survived, while my cousins did not. I think also
about what I lost. We lost forty-nine, counting first cousins. My
mother was one of nine children. With second cousins we lost eighty
relatives. I had a father, a grandmother, a lot of cousins, uncles, aunts,
and I don't even know them. My mother and I were the only ones left.
Now that my mother is gone, my shield is gone. I always think about
the Holocaust and the relatives I have never known. I wonder if my
father was standing next to his mother when she was shot?

When my mother was older, although she had all her wits about
her, she was always talking about her relatives. She has always talked a
lot about her experiences—always. Nan says that the Holocaust was
very much a continuing part of my mother's existence. After fifty
years, she was always evoking the memory of what had happened.
Nan said that they would be in the car just talking when my mother
would see a tree and say, "Umm, that would be a good place to hide."

I don't talk that much about my experiences to my children. We
have had only a few discussions. I don't want to burden them, and
I figured that she had talked with them. So my children knew from
my mother. She wanted them to know where they came from. She
never went to school, so she wanted them to know that education is

important. She also wanted them to know to be good people. My children were very close with her; she lived here. Growing up they saw her practically every day. My older son, Joel, lives around the corner, so his children also were close to her. Towards the end, my mother spent the winters in Florida, returning for Passover. In the summer, mother worked with Nan in the store in Brigantine. People loved her, and my mother loved the store.

I went back to Druysk in 1989. Before I left for the trip, my mother told me where everything was. However, no Jews are left there. Our driver spoke to some people, and they said that they had heard that Jews used to live in Druysk, but there were none left. There is still only one street. The cemetery was no longer there because a stable had been built over the cemetery. The Soviets have a law about cemeteries. If the last death had been fifty years before, it is permitted to make a park or building over the cemetery. If anyone wants to, he or she can dig up the relative's body and move this to a larger cemetery.

There were many cows and horses, a number of communal farms. The stores were leveled, except for one. That store was half the size of our former house.

I had no ties there. Our house was gone long before. The railroad does not run anymore. There was a little bus station. Some of the houses looked as if they had been redone. There are no more thatched roofs. There is electricity.

Despite the past, I am glad I ended up in the U.S. I see how I would have lived—as if in a dream. I have much more here than I would have had in Europe. I have been to Europe and once to Ponar, in 1987, when it was still under the Soviet Union, and I saw the difference.

I have a wonderful, loving family and everything I want. I don't need anything else. Most of all I have freedom.

As a young man, I did not speak of my past; however, as I have become older, I am haunted by memories. I find myself speaking of my past, especially since my mother died. She had been my shield, and when she died I began to talk more about my memories as well as those memories given to me by my mother.

I find it hard to forget my early years. In the future I hope to continue to speak to groups and continue to support and mentor public school teachers as well as those involved with teaching the Holocaust and genocide at the college and university level.

I am passionate about educating people about the *Shoah*. I do my best not to let the world forget the horror and tragedy of genocide–of the Holocaust as well as ongoing genocides of the present.

Photographs

Sara's stepmother (Esther's mother), Sara's father's third wife, who sent her to Krāslava, Latvia, after Sara's father died. The photo was found after the war. Soap had been laid on the photo.

Yankel Belak, Esther's husband, and Esther, Sara's stepsister, before the war.

Back of Yankel and Esther photograph Photographs were used in the elementary school after the war by students to do arithmetic.

Frumka Malka, Sara's sister, and Sara in front of theirs and their brother's (Matis) thatched roof home, in the 1930s, Druysk

Two aunts

Yosel and Sara Berkman 1937-1938 (the little girl is a cousin), Druysk

Aunt Sara, father's sister, and Uncle Matis, mother's older brother, before the war

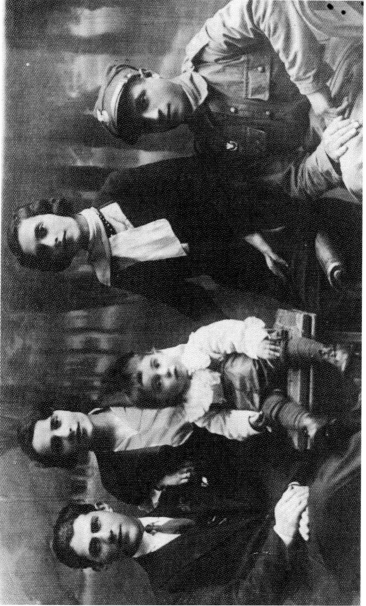

Couple, child, and Uncle Chloina, father's brother, in Polish Army uniform

Portrait of part of the Druysk townspeople: Yosel, father (last row, second from left); Sara, mother (last or second row, on right); Michel, stepfather (middle with shadow on face); Zelda and Sara Tsipa, stepsisters (first row, middle right). Of all the people in this photograph only four survived: Mother, stepfather, and stepsisters.

74

Frumka Malka (left last row) and seamstress (seated in chair), others, except the boy (the seamstress's son), are apprentices of the seamstress, pre-war, Vilna

Back of Frumka Malka photo. Photographs were used in the elementary school after the war by students to do arithmetic.

Braslav, Lithuania, 1945.   The group on its way to Poland. The Soviets would only allow Polish citizens to be repatriated.

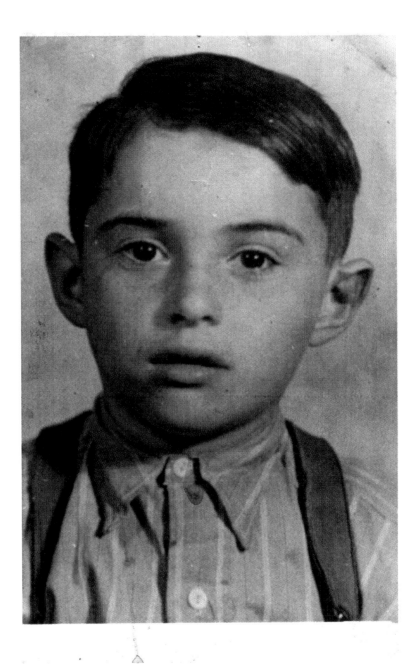

Don, ID photo, 1946, Eschwege

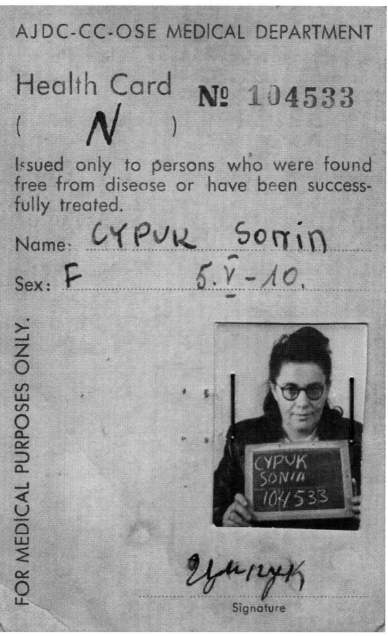

AJDC-CC-OSE MEDICAL DEPARTMENT

Health Card № 104533

(*N*)

Issued only to persons who were found
free from disease or have been successfully treated.

Name: CYPUK Sonin

Sex: F   5.V-10.

FOR MEDICAL PURPOSES ONLY.

Signature

Mother's Health Card, front, Eschwege

This is to certify that the person whose photo and signature appear overleaf passed a thorough examination including X-ray of the chest and blood serology.

The record of this examination is kept at the Area Medical Office

of ___*München*___

Date: 6.IV.49

Signature of AJDC-CC-OSE Area M.O.

Dr. Kertész László
Camp. Med. Officer
A C K 117 - Eschw

Mother's Health Card, back, Eschwege

AJDC-CC-OSE MEDICAL DEPARTMENT

Health Card   Nº 104672

(   )

Issued only to persons who were found
free from disease or have been successfully treated.

Name: _CYPUK – CHAIM_

Sex: _M._   _15.12.39_

FOR MEDICAL PURPOSES ONLY.

Signature

Don's Health Card, front, Eschwege. The birth date is incorrect.
Don's stepfather made up a date.

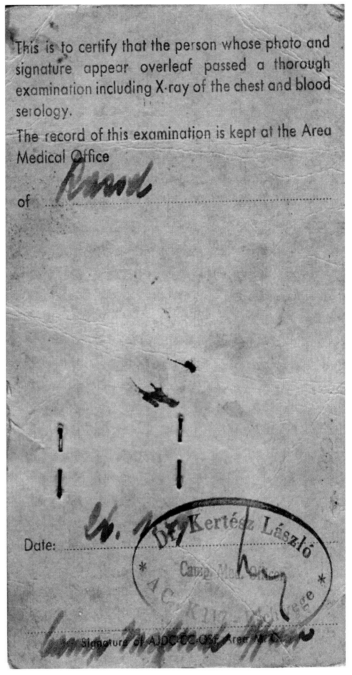

This is to certify that the person whose photo and signature appear overleaf passed a thorough examination including X-ray of the chest and blood serology.

The record of this examination is kept at the Area Medical Office

of

Date:

Signature of AJDC-CC-USE Area M.O.

Don's Health Card, back, Eschwege

Don in his first suit, Eschwege DP Camp, 1946. Michel, Don's stepfather, made the suit and shoes. HIAS gave him the material and the leather.

Marching at Eschwege DP Camp, 1947-1948, Don second from the rear

Betar Group, Eschwege, Don (second from left) displaying the Betar emblem on his sleeve; Zelda (second row, second one on right). Portraits in background: Ze'ev Jabotinsky, Theodor Herzl, Yosef Trumpeldor (See Note 31.)

Betar Group, Eschwege, Don included (first row, second from right)

86

Teacher in the middle and Don in first row, second from left

Don in new suit, 1949, St. Paul, Minnesota

Zelda (left), Mrs. Gordon (middle), Michel, stepfather (right), Don (front), 1949,
St. Paul, Minnesota

Riva, held by brother, Don, 1951, St. Paul, Minnesota

Census document

Budget Bureau Approval No. 94-R001.1
DSPC-12 (7-50)

SEMIANNUAL REPORT
OF IMMIGRANT
DISPLACED PERSONS

INSTRUCTIONS

In completing this form use a typewriter or print in ink.

Read carefully INFORMATION CONCERNING REPORTING BY IMMIGRANT DISPLACED PERSONS on this form.

If you immigrated to the United States as part of a family and were the principal applicant for immigration (the person for whom a job was assured) complete this form on reverse side for:

Yourself.
Your spouse (wife or husband), if any.
Your children who were unmarried, dependent, and under 21 years of age at time of embarkation to the United States.

If you were single and without children when you immigrated, complete this form on reverse side for yourself only.

This statement MUST BE SIGNED by the principal applicant (try the person for whom a job was assured).

Complete and mail this form to

DISPLACED PERSONS COMMISSION
% Statistical Section, Immigration and Naturalization Service
Washington 25, D. C.

Statement

I do hereby certify that the information I have provided on this form is true and correct

to the best of my knowledge.

This is my (check one):

☐ First report   ☐ Second report

☐ Third report   ☐ Fourth report

Signature of Principal Applicant (sign in ink)

Willful failure on the part of an immigrant under the Displaced Persons Act to submit an accurate report, upon conviction thereof, is subject to a fine of not more than $100 or imprisonment for not more than 6 months.

Information Concerning Reporting by Immigrant Displaced Persons

The Displaced Persons Act of 1948 requires 4 reports over a 2-year period for each eligible displaced person who immigrates to this country under Section 2 of that Act.

WHO REPORTS—The head of the family (principal applicant) reports for himself (or herself) and his (or her) spouse, and children who were unmarried, dependent and under 21 years of age at time of immigration.

A displaced person who immigrated as a single man or woman reports only for himself or herself.

HOW MANY REPORTS—A total of 4 reports is required.

WHEN IS REPORT DUE—Look below and locate the period during which you were admitted to this country. Next to it are the dates the reports are to be made.

Entered the United States	First report	Reports due Second report	Third report	Fourth report
On or before Nov. 1, 1948	Jan. 1, 1949	July 1, 1949	Jan. 1, 1950	July 1, 1950
Nov. 2, 1948 to May 1, 1949	July 1, 1949	Jan. 1, 1950	July 1, 1950	Jan. 1, 1951
May 2, 1949 to Nov. 1, 1949	Jan. 1, 1950	July 1, 1950	Jan. 1, 1951	July 1, 1951
Nov. 2, 1949 to May 1, 1950	July 1, 1950	Jan. 1, 1951	July 1, 1951	Jan. 1, 1952
May 1, 1950 to Nov. 1, 1950	Jan. 1, 1951	July 1, 1951	Jan. 1, 1952	July 1, 1952
Nov. 2, 1950 to May 1, 1951	July 1, 1951	Jan. 1, 1952	July 1, 1952	Jan. 1, 1953
On or after May 2, 1951	Jan. 1, 1952	July 1, 1952	Jan. 1, 1953	July 1, 1953

A completed report may be mailed any time within 15 days before the reporting date. For example, the January 1 report may be mailed after December 15, in time to arrive in Washington, D. C., by January 1.

REPORTING FORM—The form for reporting is provided by the Government. It will be available about a month and a half ahead of the date a report is due. For example, the form for the JANUARY 1, 1951, report will be available on or about November 15, 1950. Field offices of the U. S. Immigration and Naturalization Service will have the form on hand.

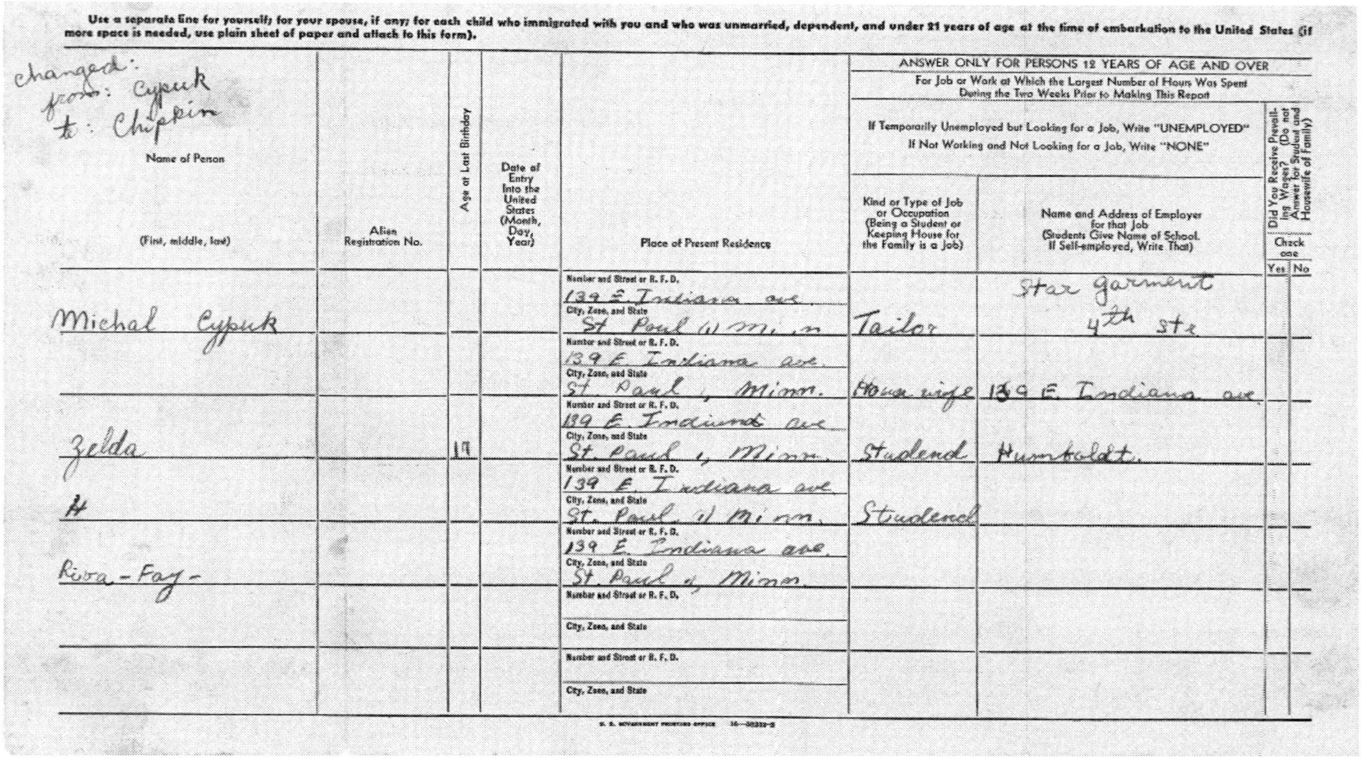

Census document

Census form (rotated). Column headers:

Name of Person (First, middle, last)	Alias Registration No.	Age at Last Birthday	Date of Entry Into the United States (Month, Day, Year)	Place of Present Residence	Kind or Type of Job or Occupation (Being a Student or Keeping House for the Family is a Job)	Name and Address of Employer (For that Job) (If Student, Give Name of School; If Self-employed, Write That)	Did You Receive Prevailing Wages? (Do not Answer for Student and Housewife of Family) Yes / No

ANSWER ONLY FOR PERSONS 12 YEARS OF AGE AND OVER
For Job or Work at Which the Largest Number of Hours Was Spent During the Two Weeks Prior to Making This Report
If Temporarily Unemployed but Looking for a Job, Write "UNEMPLOYED"
If Not Working and Not Looking for a Job, Write "NONE"
Check one

Use a separate line for yourself; for your spouse, if any; for each child who immigrated with you and who was unmarried, dependent, and under 21 years of age at the time of embarkation to the United States (if more space is needed, use plain sheet of paper and attach to this form).

Changed:
from: Cyzuck
to: Chipzin

Rows:
- Michal Cyzuck — 132 E Indiana ave, St Paul, Minn — Tailor — Star garment 47th St.
- Zelda — 139 E Indiana ave, St Paul, Minn — House wife — 139 E Indiana ave
- H — 139 E Indiana ave, St Paul, Minn — Student — Humboldt.
- Rosa – Fay — 139 E Indiana ave, St Paul, Minn — Student

U. S. GOVERNMENT PRINTING OFFICE 16-30359-2

Oceanville farmhouse, late 1950s, Riva on the porch

Sara Tsipa and David (front) Zelda (rear), Bronx, 1950s

Nan and Don's wedding photograph, August 26, 1962

Sara Berkman Chipkin, 1980

Photograph from Don's trip back to Druysk in 1993, showing the one street in the town. The sign says Druysk in Russian.

Photograph from Don's trip back to Druysk in 1993, showing the farm that was built over the Jewish cemetery

Soviet Union Trip Enables Donald Chipkin
To Visit Site of His Family's Slaughter

NE OF THE CRIME—Donald Chipkin, of Margate, on visit to the Soviet Union stands
f six pits in the Panary Forest where 100,000 Jews, including his father and entire fam
burned and the ashes scattered around the area. Only Chipkin and his mother were a
cape the clutches of the Nazis.

Logan's Bar Mitzvah, 2005. Back row: Robin (Joel's wife), Don, Nan, Joel, Michelle, Alan;
Front row: Chloe, Mason, Logan, Sara, Lanie

Czar Nicholai II Russian imperial five rouble coin

Little boy figure designed by Sara Cohen. The figure has cloth-covered buttons to symbolize the cloth-covered gold coin buttons on her grandfather's suit.

Sara Cohen's tribute to her grandfather

The childhood of Chaim Hirsh Berkman was a difficult time. He lived in Lithuania with his family which included his mother, father, grandparents, aunts, uncles, and many cousins. He had 51 relatives, but that soon changed. The Nazis invaded Lithuania and everyone in his family were killed because they were Jewish. Chaim and his mother hid from the Nazis and were not killed. They tried to escape but they were caught! They were sent to jail.

My grandfather and his mother, Sara, escaped from jail. They went to the forests to live for two years. There they found shelter and food. They ate berries, leaves, and whatever else they could find in the forest to eat so they could survive. They then lived in attics for three months. They soon went to Poland and found a monastery to live in for a while. My grandfather spoke Polish so he could pose as a Catholic boy for about three months. Soon the Russians won the war, but my Bubbie Sara did not live there because she did not want to be ruled by the Russians so they went to Germany.

Before they traveled to Germany, Sara sewed gold coin buttons that were hidden on Chaim's jacket in case they needed money. They were hidden because somebody might steal the coins. In Germany, Sara and Chaim went to a camp in Germany, Eshwega that was ruled by the Americans. They received free food and shelter. After living there for four years, they were able to get onto a boat to go to America. The reason they left Germany was because they wanted freedom, opportunity, and no discrimination.

The boat was a Navy destroyer that was used in the war. Chaim was only 8½ when they left Germany. They left on June 7, 1949. They arrived on Ellis Island on June 16, 1949. It took nine days and many people got very sick.

After leaving Ellis Island, they moved to St. Paul, Minnesota. There Chaim started school. Although he was nine, he had to start in kindergarten because he did not know how to speak English. There he got his name, Donald. He was soon able to join the other nine year old kids in third grade.

In Minnesota, his family was very poor. He needed to get a job. At nine, he worked in a junkyard taking batteries out of junk cars. Sara worked in different homes, washing floors and doing people's laundry. After living in Minnesota for five years, they moved to New Jersey where they owned an egg farm.

Donald went off to college and eventually became a pharmacist. He now lives in New Jersey with his wife Nanette. He has three children, Joel, Alan, and Michelle. He has five grandchildren, Logan, Chloe, Mason, Lanie, and Sara. Although he had a difficult childhood, he loves getting up in the morning and feels blessed to be alive because he was saved by his mother, Sara.

I, Sara Emily Cohen, was named after my Bubbe Sara.

Don in the Valley of the Lost Communities, Yad Vashem, Jerusalem, 2001. Druysk (Druisk) is engraved on the granite as well as other cities mentioned in the text: Braslaw, Slobodka, and Widze.

105

Endnotes

These "Endnotes" are not the usual notes readers see in a scholarly publication. However, I included these, and in this form, because when I was researching for this book, I learned a great deal from reading about the different subjects that I was researching. My hope is that readers of all ages will read these "Endnotes" and learn from them as I did.

—Maryann McLoughlin

Key:
En.wikipedia.org=wik
JewishGen.org=jgen
Jewishvirtuallibrary.org=jvl
Ushmm.org=ushmm

[1]**Druysk** (Rus), Drujsk (Pol), Droisk (Yid) 12 miles northeast of Bratsław, 7 miles southwest of Druya, 2 miles south of Latvian border. The Jewish population in 1897 was 515; in 1931, 412. In 1900, Druysk was part of the Russian Empire; by 1930, of Poland. —encyclopaedia judaica

[2]*Tzitzit, or tzitzis* "fringes or tassels worn by observant Jews on the corners of four-cornered garments, including the *tallit* (prayer shawl). Since they are considered by Orthodox tradition to be a time-bound commandment, they are worn only by men; Masorti (Conservative) Judaism agrees that the commandment is time-bound but regards women as exempt from wearing *tzitzit*, not as prohibited." —jvl

[3]**Misnagdim, or mitnagdim** a Hebrew word meaning "opponents," the plural of *misnaged or mitnaged*. "Most prominent among the *Misnagdim* was Rabbi Elijah (Eliyahu) ben Shlomo Zalman (1720 - 1797), commonly known as the **Vilna Gaon.** The term *Misnagdim* gained a common usage among European Jews as the term that referred to Ashkenazi religious Jews who opposed the rise and spread of early Hasidic Judaism, particularly as embodied by Hasidism's founder, Rabbi Yisrael (Israel) ben Eliezer (1698 -1760), who was known as the Baal Shem Tov.

Origins

"The rapid spread of Hasidism in the second half of the eighteenth century greatly troubled many traditional rabbis; many saw it as a potentially dangerous enemy. They felt that it was another manifestation of the recent false-messiah movement of Sabbatai Zevi (1626 - 1676) that had led many Jews astray from mainstream Judaism.

"Hasidism's founder was Rabbi Israel ben Eliezer, known as the Baal Shem Tov (master of a good name, usually applied to a saintly Jew who was also a wonder-worker), or simply the Besht; he taught that man's relationship with God depended on immediate religious experience, in addition to knowledge and observance of the details of the *Torah* and *Talmud*.

"Much of Judaism was still fearful of the pseudo-messianic movements of the Sabbateans and the Frankists (followers of the false messiah Jacob Frank (1726 -1791). Many rabbis, incorrectly as it turned out, suspected Hasidism of an intimate connection with these movements.

"The characteristically Lithuanian approach to Judaism was marked by a concentration on highly intellectual *Talmud* study. Lithuania became the heartland of the traditionalist opposition to Hasidism, to the extent that in popular perception Lithuanian and *misnaged* became virtually interchangeable terms. In fact, however, a sizable minority of Lithuanian Jews belonged to Hasidic groups, including Chabbad, Slonim, Karlin (Pinsk) and Koidanov.

Opposition of the Vilna Gaon

"The first attacks on Hasidic Judaism came during the times of the founder of Hasidic thought. Two bans of excommunication against Hasidic Jews first appeared in 1772, accompanied by the public burning of several early Hasidic pamphlets. Rabbi Elijah ben Solomon Zalman, the Vilna Gaon who galvanized opposition to Hasidic Judaism. He believed that the claims of miracles and visions made by Hasidic Jews were lies and delusions. A key point of opposition was that the Vilna Gaon maintained that greatness in Torah and observance must come through natural human efforts at *Torah* study without relying on any external miracles and wonders, whereas the Baal Shem Tov was more focused on bringing encouragement and raising the morale of the Jewish people, especially following the Chmelnitzki pogroms (1648 -1654) and the aftermath of disillusionment in the Jewish masses following the millennial excitement heightened by the failed messianic claims of Sabbatai Zevi and Jacob Frank.

"Opponents of Hasidim held that Hasidim viewed their rebbes in an idolatrous fashion.

Hasidism's changes and challenges

"Most of the changes made by the Hasidim were the product of the Hasidic approach to *Kabbalah*, particularly as expressed by Rabbi Isaac Luria (1534 - 1572), known as the ARI and his disciples, particularly Rabbi Chaim Vital (1543 - 1620). Both *Misnagdim* and *Chassidim* were greatly influenced by the ARI, but the legalistic *Misnagdim* feared in *Chassidism* what they perceived as disturbing parallels to the Sabbatean movement. An example of such an idea was the concept that the entire universe is completely nullified to God. Depending on how this idea was preached and interpreted, it could give rise to pantheism, universally acknowledged as a heresy, or lead to immoral behavior, since elements of *Kabbalah* can be misconstrued to de-emphasize ritual by rote and glorifies sexual metaphors as a deeper means of grasping some inner hidden notions in the *Torah* based on the Jews' intimate relationship with God.

"The stress of prayer over study, and the Hasidic reinterpretation of *Torah l'shma* (*Torah* study for its own sake), was seen as a rejection of the traditional Jewish views.

"Hasidim did not follow the traditional Ashkenazi prayer rite, and instead used a rite which is a combination of Ashkenazi and Sephardic rites, based upon Kabbalistic concepts from Rabbi Isaac Luria of Safed. This was seen as a rejection of the traditional Ashkenazi liturgy and, due to the resulting need for separate synagogues, a breach of communal unity.

"Hasidic Jews also added some stringencies to traditional Jewish *Halakha* on *kashrut*, the laws of keeping kosher. They made certain changes in how livestock were slaughtered and in who was considered a reliable *mashgiach* (supervisor of *kashrut*). The end result was that they essentially considered some kosher food as less stringent. This was seen as a change of traditional Judaism, an over stringency of *Halakha* (Jewish law), and, again, a breach of communal unity.

"A bitter struggle soon arose between traditional observant Jews and the newer Hasidim. At the head of the Orthodox party stood Rabbi Elijah ben Solomon. In 1772, when the first secret circles of Hasidim appeared in Lithuania, the rabbinic *kahal* (council) of Vilna, with the approval of Rabbi Elijah ben Solomon, arrested the local leaders of the sect, and excommunicated its adherents. Letters were sent from Vilna to the rabbis of other communities calling upon them to make war upon the godless sect.

"In many places persecutions were instituted against the Hasidim. The appearance in 1780 of the first works of Hasidic literature created alarm among the Orthodox. At the council of rabbis held in the village of Zelva, Trakai Voivodeship, in 1781, it was resolved to uproot Hasidism. In the official letters issued by the council, the faithful were ordered to expel the Hasidim from every Jewish community, to regard them as members of another faith, to hold no social intercourse with them, not to intermarry with them, and not to bury their dead.

"Hasidism in the south of eastern Europe had established itself so firmly in the various communities that it had no fear of persecution. The main sufferers were the northern Hasidim. Their leader, Hasidic Rabbi Shneur Zalman of Liadi (1745 -1812), the founder of *Chabbad Hasidism*, attempted to allay the anger of the *Mitnagdim* and of Elijah Gaon.

"On the death of the latter in 1797 the exasperation of the *Mitnagdim* became so great that they resolved to libel and denounce the leaders of the Hasidim to the Russian government as dangerous agitators and teachers of heresy. In consequence twenty-two Hasidic Jews were arrested in Vilna and other places. Rabbi Shneur Zalman of Liadi was arrested at his court in Liozna and brought to St. Petersburg (1798). Chabbad Hasidim still celebrate the day of his liberation from prison and they still regard the *mitnagdim* with great contempt for what they deem as the betrayal of their first rebbe.

"The struggle of *Misnagdim* with Hasidism in Lithuania and White Russia led to the formation of the latter sect in those regions into separate religious organizations; these existing in many towns alongside of those of the Mitnagdim. In the south-western region the Hasidim almost completely crowded out the Mitnagdim. Lithuania remained strongly Mitnagdic. Another group of non-Hasidic Jews were the Oberlander Jews of Hungary and Slovakia, who were not always considered to be Misnagdim.

"By the mid-1800s most of non-Hasidic Judaism had discontinued its struggle with Hasidism and had reconciled itself to the establishment of the latter as a fact.

"The Israeli historian Jacob Katz has documented how other practices provocatively separated the Hasidim from their neighbors. For example, Hasidim advocated using a sharper knife when slaughtering animals than the one used by the Mitnagdim's slaughterers. Such stringency had a socially divisive effect: The Hasidim no longer could eat at the Mitnagdim's houses. The Hasidim also adopted a different prayer book, so that their synagogue service differed somewhat from that of other Jews and had to be conducted separately. Their most brilliant act of public relations was labeling themselves Hasidim, the Hebrew word for both pious and saintly, while calling their adversaries Mitnagdim, Hebrew for "opponents." These terms made the Hasidim seem like the more dynamic and positive of the two groups.

"With the passage of time, the Hasidim and Mitnagdim recognized that their differences were increasingly inconsequential, particularly after both groups found themselves facing a common enemy: the nineteenth century Haskalah, or Jewish Enlightenment. Jewish parents, who once feared that their Hasidic or Mitnagdim child might go over to the other camp, were now far more afraid that their child might become altogether irreligious.

"An additional factor that lessened the HasidicMitnagdim split was nineteenth and twentieth century Hasidism's increasing emphasis on Talmud study. As the movement expanded, it put less emphasis on meditation and communing with God, and more on traditional Jewish learning. As a result, Hasidim today are no longer regarded as revolutionaries; in fact, they are the conservative stalwarts of Orthodox Judaism, easily recognized by the eighteenth and nineteenth century black coats and hats worn by most of their male adherents.

"Nonetheless, the Hasidic approach to Judaism significantly differs from that of the Mitnagdim. Hasidism generally places a much greater stress on *simcha shel mitzvah* — the joy of performing a commandment." —wik; jvl

[4]**Flax** (also known as common flax or linseed) (binomial name: *Linum usitatissimum*) is a "member of the *genus Linum* in the family *Linaceae*. It is native to the region extending from the eastern Mediterranean to India and was probably first domesticated in the Fertile Crescent. This is called as Jawas/Javas or Alashi in Marathi. Flax was extensively cultivated in ancient Egypt. (New Zealand flax is not related to flax, but was named after it as both plants are used to produce fibers.)

"Flax is an erect annual plant growing to 1.2 m tall, with slender stems. The leaves are glaucous green, slender lanceolate, 20–40 mm long and 3 mm broad. The flowers are pure pale blue, 15–25 mm diameter, with five petals; they can also be bright red. The fruit is a round, dry capsule 5–9 mm diameter, containing several glossy brown seeds shaped like an apple pip, 4–7 mm long.

"In addition to referring to the plant itself, "flax" may refer to the unspun fibers of the flax plant. Flax fibers are amongst the oldest fiber crops in the world. The use of flax for the production of linen goes back 5000 years. Pictures on tombs and temple walls at Thebes depict flowering flax plants. The use of flax fibre in the manufacturing of cloth in northern Europe dates back to Neolithic times. In North America, flax was introduced by the Puritans. Currently most flax produced in the USA and Canada is seed flax types for the production of linseed oil or flaxseeds for human nutrition."—wik

[5]**Flu** "Is it possible that a poorly adapted H1N1 virus was already beginning to spread in 1915, causing some serious illnesses but not yet sufficiently fit to initiate a pandemic? Data consistent with this possibility were reported at the time from European military camps. Whether the epidemic recognized as Spanish flu in Europe in the summer of 1918 was caused by a similarly conserved virus is unknown, and whether anecdotal cases and outbreaks reported from Europe in 1916 and 1917 and the United States in early 1918 were caused by a virus related to the pandemic virus remains speculative. The 1915/1916 influenza epidemic was noted at the time as the worst to date that century. The 1915/1916 and 1916/1917 influenza seasons and in January 1918, excess mortality incidence was greatest in those ≥65 years old. During February-April 1918 and the 1918/1919 season, those ≥65 years old experienced little or no excess mortality, whereas those aged 15-24 and 25-44 years experienced sharply elevated death rates. . . . .

"Further analysis of age-detailed historical mortality data from other regions and periods may continue to provide insight into the epidemiology of past influenza pandemics and may help to inform current preparedness planning efforts for future pandemics. The historical-epidemiological evidence of the precursor wave that we present, along with a recent study of transmissibility in the pandemic wave of autumn 1918, suggest that if events similar to those preceding autumn 1918 were to occur again, strengthened surveillance and increased capacity for rapid public health intervention could possibly prove critical in limiting the emergence and impact of the next pandemic. The speed with which human-to-human transmissibility of a highly pathogenic mammalian adapted avian influenza virus develops cannot currently be predicted. Nevertheless, the historical precedent of 20th-century influenza pandemics suggests that theoretically controllable transmissibility and a herald wave may occur before the onset of a catastrophic pandemic wave, leaving a critical window of opportunity for production and distribution of pandemic vaccines and antivirals." www.pnas.org; www.cdc.gov/ncidod/eid/vol12no01

[6]**Kraslava, Latvia** "During 1920–1935 the number of Jews in the cities of Latvia increased from 24,000 to 44,000. According to official statistics, Latvian Jews numbered 95,675, or 5.2% of the total population in 1925, and 41% Jews lived in Riga, where over one fourth of all commercial and industrial enterprises were owned by Jews.

"Inter-war Latvia, as well as in the other two Baltic States, was a comparatively pleasant place for Jews to live in. The right-wing takeover by Karlis Ulmanis regime in 1934 was not accompanied by anti-Jewish violence, however the new government made efforts to nationalize the economy, with negative consequences for Jews. Jewish community life was interrupted by Soviet occupation in 1940, followed by the tragedy of Holocaust." —jgen

[7]**Shoemakers** Because we have available to us so many inexpensive shoes, we may not realize the value of shoes in other times and places. In the early to mid 20th century, many shoes were still made by hand. The upper portion was made by an "uppers" maker, or cordwainer. A shoebinder bound the uppers to the soles. The sole portion was made by a maker of soles or one who bottomed shoes. There was also the person who repaired soles. Because of the handwork, shoes were very expensive; boots even more so. —From Blevett, Mary H. *Men, Women, and Work: Class, Gender, and Protest in The New England Shoe Industry 1780-1910.*

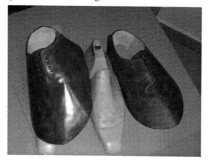

A finished upper handmade shoes.wordpress

[8]*Kristallnacht* On November 9, 1938, the Nazis unleashed a wave of pogroms against Germany's Jews. "In the space of a few hours, thousands of synagogues and Jewish businesses and homes were damaged or destroyed. This event came to be called *Kristallnacht* (Night of Broken Glass) for the shattered store windowpanes that carpeted German streets. [But the night was much more than 'broken glass.']

"The pretext for this violence was the November 7 assassination of a German diplomat in Paris, Ernst vom Rath, by Herschel Grynszpan, a Jewish teenager whose parents, along with 17,000 other Polish Jews, had been recently expelled from the Reich. Though portrayed as spontaneous outbursts of popular outrage, these pogroms were calculated acts of retaliation carried out by the SA, SS, and local Nazi party organizations.

"Storm troopers killed at least 91 Jews and injured many others. For the first time, Jews were arrested on a massive scale and transported to Nazi concentration camps. About 30,000 Jews were sent to Buchenwald, Dachau, and Sachsenhausen, where hundreds died within weeks of arrival. Release came only after the prisoners arranged to emigrate and agreed to transfer their property to 'Aryans.'

"*Kristallnacht* culminated the escalating violence against Jews that began during the incorporation of Austria into the Reich in March 1938. It also signaled the fateful transfer of responsibility for 'solving' the 'Jewish Question' to the SS." —ushmm

[9]**Nazi-Soviet Pact** "The Molotov-Ribbentrop Pact, also known as the Hitler-Stalin Pact or Ribbentrop-Molotov Pact or Nazi-Soviet Pact and formally known as the Treaty of Nonaggression between Germany and the Union of Soviet Socialist Republics, was in theory a non-aggression treaty between the German Third Reich and the Soviet Union. It was signed in Moscow on August 23, 1939, by the Soviet foreign minister Vyacheslav Molotov and the German foreign minister Joachim von Ribbentrop. The mutual non-aggression treaty lasted until *Operation Barbarossa* of June 22, 1941, when Nazi Germany invaded the Soviet Union.

"Although officially labeled a 'non-aggression treaty,' the pact included a secret protocol, in which the independent countries of Finland, Estonia, Latvia, Lithuania, Poland, and Romania were divided into the spheres of interest of the [two countries]. The secret protocol explicitly assumed 'territorial and political rearrangements' in the areas of these countries, which practically rendered it into an aggressive military alliance, in spite of its official name. Subsequently all the mentioned countries were invaded by the Soviets, the Nazis, or both. Only Finland, which fought twice against the Soviet Union in WWII, successfully resisted conquest, but was forced to concede territory." —wik

[10]**Operation Barbarossa** "On December 18, 1940, Hitler signed War Directive No. 21 to the German high command for an operation now codenamed Operation Barbarossa stating: 'The German Wehrmacht must be prepared to crush Soviet Russia in a quick campaign.' The operation was named after the Emperor Frederick Barbarossa of the Holy Roman Empire, a leader of the Third Crusade in the 12th century.

"Germany adhered to their non-aggression pact with Russia for the first two years of WWII. Once the Nazis withdrew from the Battle of Britain, however, their attention turned to the East. At 04:00 hours, on June 22, 1941, Adolf Hitler launched the greatest land-air attack in the history of war—*Operation Barbarossa*. The assault was comprised of 3 million troops, 3,500 tanks, and 1,800 aircraft.

"Hitler's generals advised him against waging war on two fronts, especially since the Red Army was far superior in number, but Hitler pressed ahead regardless. The German advance was swift at first—200 miles in the first week. In July, the city of Smolensk had been secured and Leningrad (now St Petersburg) was under siege soon after. By September, the city of

Kiev had fallen with 650,000 Russian soldiers—the most prisoners ever taken in battle.

"By the end of the year, more than 3 million Russians had been taken prisoner and another million were dead. The Nazis had the Kremlin in their sights. Hitler expected Moscow to fall quickly. However, fierce resistance drove the Germans back into the icy plains. His army was left out in the bitter cold, without the resources for winter warfare. This grueling war of attrition ground on until July 1943, when Germany was finally beaten.

"Ambitious from the start, *Operation Barbarossa's* failure marked a downturn for the Nazi's fortunes. But Russia's victory came at a massive price. Up to 28 million
Russians perished during WWII—most of them during this brutal chapter."
—discoverychannel.co.uk

[11]**Ernst Busch** "born in Essen-Steele, Germany, on 6th July, 1885. After being educated at Gross Lichterfelde Cadet Academy he joined the German Army in 1904 and during the First World War served on the Western Front where he fought at Arras and Verdun. In 1918 he won the *Pour le Mérite* for showing exceptional courage during battle.

"Busch remained in the army and in 1925 was appointed Inspector of Transport Troops and in 1930 was promoted to the rank of lieutenant colonel and placed in command of the 9th Infantry Regiment.

"An ardent supporter of the Nazi Party, Busch achieved rapid promotion after Adolf Hitler came to power in 1933. Within two years he had been promoted to major general and was commander of the 23rd Infantry Division. In February 1938 Hitler appointed him general. Whereas most senior officers pleaded with Hitler to move with caution, Busch and fellow Nazi, Walther von Reichenau, urged him to invade Czechoslovakia.

"Busch served under Siegmund List during the invasion of Poland in September 1939. The following year he led the 16th Army during the Western Offensive. On the 26th May, 1940, Hitler awarded him the Knight's Cross.

"Busch took part in *Operation Barbarossa* and on 8th September 1941 his 16th Army took Demyansk before taking part in the siege of Leningrad. Despite a counter-attack by the Red Army Busch's troops held the line from Staraya to Ostashkov. After a brave defense of his position he was promoted to field marshal.

"In October 1943 Busch replaced General Gunther von Kluge as head of Army Group Centre. However, he only held the post until June 1944 when he was replaced by General Walther Model.

"Busch was recalled in March 1945 when he became head of Army Group Northwest. Along with Kurt Student and his 1st Parachute Army, Busch had the task of trying to halt the advance of General Bernard Montgomery and the Allies into Germany.

"Ernst Busch, who surrendered on 3rd May, 1945. He was taken to Britain as a prisoner of war and he died in captivity on 17th July 1945."
—www.spartacus.schoolnet.co.uk/2WWbusch.

[12] **Kovno** "Between the World Wars industry prospered in Kovno (Kaunas), as it was the largest city in Lithuania. In 1940 it was annexed by the Soviet Union into the Lithuanian SSR. The Jewish population of Kovno 37,000 people, was attacked by anti-Communist Lithuanian partisans, killing 3,800 people (see the Jager Report), and some of these massacres were even filmed. Under German occupation 1941-1944 most of the remaining Jewish population was confined in the Kaunas Ghetto (also known as the Kauen Concentration Camp), and many were shot at the Ninth Fort. Only 3,000 or so Jews survived the war." —wik

[13]**Ninth Fort** "At the end of 19th century, the city of Kaunas was fortified, and by 1890 it was encircled by eight forts and nine gun batteries. The construction of the Ninth Fort (its numerical designation having stuck as a proper noun) began in 1902 and was completed on the eve of the First World War. From 1924-on, the Ninth Fort was used as the city of Kaunas' prison.

"During the years of Soviet occupation, 1940-1941, the Ninth Fort was used by the NKVD to house political prisoners on their way to the gulags of Siberia.

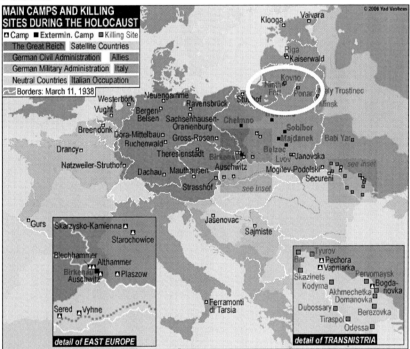

Ninth Fort and Ponar circled.

"During the years of Nazi occupation, the Ninth Fort was put to use as a place of mass murder. At least 5,000 Lithuanian Jews of Kaunas, largely taken from the city's Jewish ghetto, were transported to the Ninth Fort and killed. In addition, Jews from as far as France, Austria and Germany were

114

brought to Kaunas during the course of Nazi occupation and executed in the Ninth Fort. In 1944, as the Soviets moved in, the Germans liquidated the ghetto and what had by then come to be known as the 'Fort of Death,' and the prisoners were dispersed to other camps. After the Second World War, the Soviets again used the Ninth Fort as a prison for several years. From 1948 to 1958, farm organizations were run out of the Ninth Fort.

"In 1958, a museum was established in the Ninth Fort. In 1959, a first exposition was prepared in four cells telling about Nazi war crimes carried out throughout Lithuania. In 1960, the discovery, cataloguing, and forensic investigation of local mass murder sites began in an effort to gain knowledge regarding the scope of these crimes." —wik

Einsatzgruppen (mobile killing squads). Circled area is Druysk and Vilna/Ponar.

[14]**Vidzy** Prior to World War I, Vidzy was part of the Russian Empire; It became part of Poland in 1920. 1939 the Soviet entered; then they gave it to Lithuania. In 1941 Nazi Germany took over, and Vidzy was incorporated into Belarus (under the Soviets) in 1945. Today it is in the Northwest part of Belarus near the Lithuania and Latvian border. (See map in Map section.)

"Throughout history, Widze, often spelled Vidzy, was regarded as one of the four largest market places in Lithuania. Established over 500 years ago in the Lithuanian kingdom, its history was marked by numerous wars: Russians vs. Swedes; Lithuanians vs. Poles; Germans vs. Russians. Prior to World War I, it belonged to Russia; afterwards, it became Poland. During World War II, again Russia, then Lithuania, later Nazi Germany, and finally it was incorporated into Belarus. The same fate was shared by many towns

in the Vilna district. Widze was destroyed numerous times, in various wars and by fire. It happened twice in the lifetime of the previous generation. At the beginning of the First World War, battles in the area forced nearly the entire Jewish population to flee. About fifty who remained were subjected to persecution, torture and rape, while most of the town was left in ruins. After the war, less than half of the previous population of about 4,000 Jews gradually returned to rebuild their lives and the Jewish community. The last destruction began with the invasion of the Germans in June 1941, which culminated with the final chapter of the Widze ghetto, as the remaining survivors were transported to their death in the Ponar woods near Vilna on April 5, 1943. In the early 1990's there remained one old Jewish woman in town and she would not identify herself as a Jew."
—From Winer, Gershon. "Kaddish for Our *Shtetl*." Yizkor. —jgen

Deportation "In the winter of 1942 the Nazis announced that the Jews of Slobodka and Druysk must leave their houses and must move to the city of Vidzy and to the Ghetto of Braslav. Sleighs driven by local peasants arrived and Gentile neighbors gathered around, gleefully waiting the departure of the Jews and the opportunity to grab their property.

"The ride to Vidzy passed through Braslav, where the Jews were locked in a ghetto. The peasant drivers warned that pits had been dug behind Braslav ready for the Jews. Still some stopped in Braslav where they would share the fate of its Jews. Others, including Boris Berkman, used a moment when the guards were less attentive to jump from the sleigh and escape. Most, however, reached Vidzy, where they were housed in overcrowded conditions in the Synagogue and the Beth Midrash of the ghetto together with other Jews who had been transferred from Druysk, Dubinova, and Plussy. The local *Judenrat* managed to organize work for most of the remaining Jews, especially to cut peat from the bogs near Opsa and in various workshops.

The End Game
"Shortly the ghetto was surrounded by Lithuanian collaborators belonging to the *ypatingasis burys* death squads who were responsible for most of the executions of Jews in the Vilna area. Those deemed useful for work were distributed to work camps in Estonia and Latvia.

Swieciany "Most of the 1300 surviving Jews in Vidzy were transferred to the small ghetto in Swieciany (Svintsyan, Svencionys), where they were crowded into local community buildings together with other Jews from some twenty communities.

"The lack of food and poor sanitary conditions led to the outbreak of typhus which took many. In March 1943 SS-*Sturmbannführer* Horst Wulff, the Nazi *Gebeitskommissar* of Vilna-Land (the district surrounding the city), decided to clear all the remaining ghettos in the Belarusian-Latvian border lands, ostensibly due to acute rise in Partisan activity in the area fueled by escapees from the ghettos. The head of the Vilna *Judenrat*, Jacob Gens, was brought to Swieciany to inform the Jews that those with useful professions for the Germans were to be moved to Vilna, while the others were be

116

transported to Kovno. Salek Dressler, the commander of the Vilna Jewish Police, arrived in the ghetto to arrange the transfer. Still panic spread though the community, as everybody understood from previous experience that it was important to be included among the group considered 'useful.'

"On April 4, all the Jews gathered at the station in Nowo-Swieciany and boarded the freight wagons under the guard of the Vilna Jewish Police. Gens realizing too late that the operation was a Nazi charade, arranged for five hundred Jews, including the families of the Swieciany *Judenrat*, were dropped off in Vilna. The remaining wagons were detained at the station while the Nazis were busy murdering the Jews from the Ghetto of Sol. The following day the Gestapo and Lithuanian police took control of the train and detoured from the route to Kovno to Ponar, the mass murder site of the Jews of the Ghetto Vilna. On arrival at Ponar the Jews realized that they had been tricked. They burst from the locked cars and a mass breakout ensued. Six hundred Jews were slain from indiscriminate fire to control the flight with bodies littering the depot and the surrounding fields. Some resisted and a number of Germans and Lithuanian collaborators were also killed. The majority were captured and led to the Ponar death pits where the Jews of Swieciany, Vidzy, Druysk and Slobodka were murdered by the Lithuanian Police volunteers of *ypagtingasis burys* death squads led by Lt. Balys Norvaisca and Lt. Balys Lukoschos under command of SS-*Hauptsturmfuhrer* Martin Weiss from Gestapo Department 4 of the Security Police (Sipo) in Vilna.

"On April 6, Weiss ordered 25 Jewish Policemen from Vilna to accompany him to Ponar to collect the bodies the lay strewn in woods and fields and bury the dead in the pits." —www.seligman.org.il/slobodka_ holocaust.html

[15]**Ponar** "In 1944, at the Ponary execution site, Szloma Gol was among seventy Jews, and ten Russian prisoners of war suspected of being Jewish, who as members of a *Blobel Kommando*, had to dig up and then burn the bodies of those who had been murdered during the years 1941–1943.

"Each night the eighty prisoners were forced to sleep in a deep pit to which the only access was by a ladder drawn up each evening. Each morning, chained at the ankles and waist, they were put to work to dig up and burn tens of thousands of corpses.

"These eighty prisoners were supervised by thirty Lithuanian and German guards and fifty SS men. Their guards were armed with pistols, daggers, and automatic guns—one armed guard for each chained prisoner.

"Two and a half years later Szloma Gol recalled how, between the end of September 1943, when their work began, and April 1944:

> We dug up altogether 68,000 corpses. I know this because two of the Jews in the pit with us were ordered by the Germans to keep count of the bodies—that was their sole job. The bodies were mixed, Jews, Polish priests, Russian prisoners-of-war.

Amongst those that I dug up I found my own brother. I found his identification papers on him. He had been dead two years when I dug him up, because I know that he was in a batch of 10,000 Jews from the Vilna ghetto who were shot in September 1941.

The Jews worked in chains, anyone removing the chains, they were warned, would be hanged. As they worked, the guards beat and stabbed them. "I was once knocked senseless on to the pile of bodies," Szloma Gol recalled," and could not get up, but my companions took me off the pile." Then I "went sick."

"Prisoners were allowed to go sick for two days, staying in the pit while the others worked. On the third day, if they were still too sick to work, they would be shot. Szloma Gol managed to return to work.

"As the digging up and burning of the bodies proceeded, eleven of the eighty Jews were shot by the guards – sadistic acts which gratified the killers, and were intended to terrorize and cow the prisoners.

"But inside the pit, a desperate plan of escape was being put into effect – the digging of a tunnel from the bottom of the pit to a point beyond the camp wire, at the edge of the Ponary woods.

"While the tunnel was still being dug, a Czech SS man alerted the Jews to their imminent execution, 'They are going to shoot you soon,' he told them, and 'they are going to shoot me too, and put us all on the pile. Get out if you can, but not while I am on guard.'

"One of the sixty-nine surviving prisoners, Isaac Dogim, took the lead on organizing the escape. Dogim had been placing the corpses in layers on the pyre one day, when he recognized his wife, his three sisters, and his three nieces.

"All the bodies were decomposed, he recognized his wife by the medallion that he had given her on their wedding day. Another prisoner, Yudi Farber, who had been a civil engineer before the war, joined in the preparations for the escape.

"On 15 April 1944 the prisoners in the pit at Ponary made their bid for freedom. Forty of them managed to get through the tunnel, but a guard, alerted by the sound of footsteps on the pine branches, opened fire.

"In the ensuing chase twenty- five Jews were shot, but fifteen managed to reach the woods, later most of them joined the partisans in the distant Rudniki forest.

"Five days after the escape, the remaining twenty-nine prisoners were shot." —www.holocaustresearchproject.org/einsatz/ponary.html

Ponary, 1944. Ladders were pulled up each night, so laborers could not escape.

[16]**Braslav** (Pol. Brasław), small town in Belarus; in Poland until 1795 and between 1921 and 1939.

The Holocaust Period

"In 1941, on the eve of the Holocaust, there were 2,500 Jews in Braslav.

The city was captured by the Germans on June 28, 1941, and on the following day the German army and police removed all the city's Jews to the nearby swamp area, where they were held for two days. Meanwhile, all Jewish property had been stolen by the local population. On August 2, 1941, a 'contribution' of 100,000 rubles was demanded of the Jews. At the beginning of April 1942, a ghetto was established, and, in addition to the local Jewish population, Jews from Dubinovo, Druya, Druysk, Miory, and Turmont were interned there. The population of the ghetto was divided into two parts: the workers and the 'nonproductive.' In the first *Aktion* – on June 3–5, 1942 – about 3,000 people were killed; local farmers actively helped the Germans in this *Aktion*. After some of the Jews went into hiding, the German commander announced that those Jews who came out of hiding of their own free will would not be harmed, but the handful who responded to this call were executed on June 7. In the autumn of 1942, the ghetto was turned into a work camp in which the remainder of the Jews were concentrated. On March 19, 1943, the Nazis began to liquidate the camp, but this time they met with opposition. A group of Jews, fortified in one of the buildings, offered armed resistance. Only after their ammunition ran out did the Nazis succeed in suppressing the opposition. The fighters fell at their posts. There were 40 survivors of the Braslav community, some of whom fought in partisan units in the area. After the war a monument was erected to the Jews killed there by the Nazis. In 1970 there were 18 Jewish families with no synagogue." — Aharon Weiss, jvl

[17]**Babi Yar** "By 1941, the focus and function of the *Einsatzgruppen* had changed significantly. With the initiation of Operation Barbarossa, Germany's assault on the Soviet Union, the mobile killing units operated over a wide area of Eastern Europe from the Baltic to the Black Sea. There were four main divisions of the Einsatzgruppen — Groups A, B, C and D. These groups, all under Heydrich's general command, operated just behind the advancing German troops eliminating undesirables: political criminals, Polish governmental officials, gypsies and, mostly, Jews. Jews were rounded up in every village, transported to a wooded area, or a ravine (either natural or constructed by Jewish labor). They (men, women and children) were stripped, shot and buried. Sachar provides a description of one of the most brutal mass exterminations — at a ravine named Babi Yar, near the Ukrainian city of Kiev:

> Kiev ... contained a Jewish population of 175,000 on the eve of the Nazi invasion of the Soviet Union in 1941. The Nazi forces captured the city in mid-September; within less than a fortnight, on the 29th. and 30th., nearly 34,000 Jews of the ghetto were brought to a suburban ravine known as Babi Yar, near the Jewish Cemetery, where men, women, and children were systematically machine-gunned in a two-day orgy of execution. In subsequent months, most of the remaining population was exterminated.
>
> This, the most appalling massacre of the war, is often alluded to as a prime example of utter Jewish helplessness in the face of disaster. But even the few desperate attempts, almost completely futile, to strike back served as a reminder that the difference between resistance and submission depended very largely upon who was in possession of the arms that back up the will to do or die. The Jews in their thousands, with such pathetic belongings as they could carry, were herded into barbed-wire areas at the top of the ravine, guarded by Ukrainian collaborators. There they were stripped of their clothes and beaten, then led in irregular squads down the side of the ravine. The first groups were forced to lie on the ground, face down, and were machine-gunned by the Germans who kept up a steady volley.
>
> The riddled bodies were covered with thin layers of earth and the next groups were ordered to lie over them, to be similarly dispatched. To carry out the murder of 34,000 human beings in the space of two days could not assure that all the victims had died. Hence there were a few who survived and, though badly wounded, managed to crawl from under the corpses and seek a hiding place.
>
> After the main massacre, the site was converted into a more permanent camp to which thousands of victims from other parts of the Ukraine could be sent for extermination. It became

known as the Syrets camp, taking its name from a nearby Kiev neighborhood. Several hundred selected prisoners were quartered there -- carpenters, shoemakers, tailors, and other artisans — to serve the needs of the SS men and the Ukrainian guards. They were usually killed within a few weeks and replaced by others who continued their duties. In charge of the administration and ultimate killing was Paul von Radomski, who seemed to crave a reputation for outdoing his sadist colleagues in other camps." — jvl —See also the poem "Babi Yar," by Yevgeni Yevtushenko, 1961.

[18]**Cordwainer or Cobbler** The name for a shoemaker originally was cordwainer. "One distinction preserved by cordwainers since the earliest times is, that a cordwainer works only with new leather, where a cobbler works with old. Cobblers have always been repairers, frequently prohibited by law from actually making shoes. Even going so far as to collect worn-out footwear, cut it apart, and remanufacture cheap shoes entirely form salvaged leather, cobblers have contended with cordwainers since at least the Middle Ages." See note 7. —www.bastonfamily.co.uk

[19]*Sonderkommandos* "At Auschwitz, Treblinka, Birkenau, Belzec, Chelmno and Sobibor, the Nazis established the *Sonderkommando*, groups of Jewish male prisoners picked for their youth and relative good health whose job was to dispose of corpses from the gas chambers or crematoria. Some did the work to delay their own deaths; some thought they could protect friends and family, and some acted out of mere greed for extra food and money these men sometimes received. The men were forced into this position, with the only alternative being death in the gas chambers or being shot on the spot by an SS guard.

"At Auschwitz, the *Sonderkommandos* had better physical conditions than other inmates; they had decent food, slept on straw mattresses and could wear normal clothing. *Sonderkommandos* were divided into several groups, each with a specialized function. Some greeted the new arrivals, telling them that they were going to shower prior to being sent to work. They were obliged to lie, telling the soon-to-be-murdered prisoners that after the delousing process they would be assigned to labor teams and reunited with their families. These were the only *Sonderkommandos* to have contact with the victims while they were still alive. The SS carried out the gassings, and the *Sonderkommandos* would enter the chambers afterward, remove the bodies, process them and transport them to the crematorium. Other teams processed the corpses after the gas chambers, extracting gold teeth, and removing clothes and valuables before taking them to the crematoria for final disposal. The remains were ground to dust and mixed with the ashes. When too much ash mounted, the *Sonderkommandos*, under the watchful eyes of the SS, would throw them into a nearby river.

"At Treblinka about 200 men were in charge of removing the corpses from the gas chambers. At Auschwitz the *Sonderkommando* working in the crematoria initially numbered 400 men, but the number was raised during the mass murder of Hungarians in 1944 to about 1,000 men. At Auschwitz and Birkenau, the *Sonderkommando* were responsible for sorting the suitcases, packages and other items with which the prisoners arrived on the trains. These items were taken to a storage area of the camp euphemistically called 'Canada,' where the 'Clearing Commando' would unpack them, sort them, and prepare them for dispatch to Germany.

"Despite the better conditions in which the *Sonderkommando* lived at the camps, most were eventually gassed as they became increasingly weak or sick from camp conditions. The Nazis also did not want any evidence of their horrific acts to remain, and therefore decided to kill those prisoners who witnessed their actions.

"In October 1944, the *Sonderkommando* team at Birkenau learned that the Germans intended to gas them. At the camps, an underground movement had been planning a general uprising for some time, but it never happened. The remaining *Sonderkommandos* decided to take their fate into their own hands, and, on October 7, the group in charge of the third crematorium at the camp, the Birkenau Three *Sonderkommando*, rebelled. They attacked the SS with makeshift weapons: stones, axes, hammers, other work tools and homemade grenades. They caught the SS guards by surprise, overpowered them and blew up a crematorium. At this stage they were joined by the Birkenau One *Kommando*, which also overpowered their guards and broke out of the compound. The revolt ended in failure. There was no mass uprising, and within a short time the Germans succeeded in capturing and killing almost all the escapees.

"The *Sonderkommandos* tend to be regarded very negatively by most survivors and to a certain extent the Jewish establishment in general. In the camps, the *Sonderkommandos* were seen as unclean, and the writer Primo Levi described them as being 'akin to collaborators.' He said that their testimonies should not be given much credence, 'since they had much to atone for and would naturally attempt to rehabilitate themselves at the expense of the truth.' Those who were members of the *Sonderkommando*, however, state they had no choice in their job, and they were as much victims of Nazi oppression as other prisoners in the concentration camps."

—"*Sonderkommandos*," Jacqueline Shields, jvl

20Coal tar soap Wright's Coal Tar Soap "Created by William Valentine Wright in 1860, Wright's Traditional Soap, or Wright's Coal Tar Soap, is a popular brand of antiseptic soap that is designed to thoroughly cleanse the skin. It is an orange color.

Coal Tar Soap logo

"For over 130 years, Wright's Coal Tar Soap was a popular brand of household soap; it can still be bought in supermarkets and chemists worldwide. It was developed by William Valentine Wright Jr. in 1866 from 'liquor carbonis detergens,' the liquid by-product of the distillation of coal to make coke; the liquid was made into an antiseptic soap for the treatment of skin diseases.

History

"WV Wright was a wholesale druggist and chemist who had a small business at 11 Old Fish Street Hill, Doctors Commons, London. Now non-existent, Old Fish Street Hill near St Paul's Cathedral was the 14th century fish market, before Billingsgate). WV Wright Jr. was born in Clapham, the son of William Valentine Wright senior. WV Wright developed a reputation with his recipe for non-alcoholic communion wine. The business can be traced back to that of James Curtis & Co, a wholesale druggist in 1795. In 1867, WV Wright, Jr. moved his firm, Wright, Sellers & Layman, to small (one-third acre) premises at 50 Southwark Street, Southwark, London. This area of London was already renowned for its glue factories and tanneries. WV Wright Jr. died in 1913.

"In June 1899 Wright, Layman & Umney became a private limited company with a capital of £100,000 (about $15 million in today's terms) with Charles Umney as Director.

"During the first year of trading as a public limited company in 1899, product range was enlarged to include Wright's Coal Tar Shaving Soap in powder form.

"Readers of the *Country-Side* magazine in 1906 were offered the chance to buy an inexpensive cabinet frame for one shilling, in which they could stack twelve empty Wright's Coal Tar Soap packets to act as sliding drawers in a cabinet for natural history specimens. As the editorial mentioned: 'the measurements have been chosen because so many of our readers are users of Wright's Coal Tar Soap.' Wright's Coal Tar Soap was a regular advertiser in the magazine.

"In the late 1960s the Wright's Coal Tar Soap business was taken over by LRC Products Ltd (London International Group) who sold it to Smith & Nephew in the 1990s.

"The soap is now made by Accantia and is called Wright's Traditional Soap. As European Union directives on cosmetics have banned the use of coal-tar in non-prescription products, the coal tar derivates have been removed from the formula, replacing them with tea tree oil as main anti-bacterial ingredient. Despite this major

variance from the original recipe, the new soap has been made to look and smell like the original product, despite differing substantially in composition." —wik

[21]**Black "drawing" salve** "Ichthammol is aluminum bituminosulphate. It is distilled from high sulphur oil shale. It has more in common with coal tar shampoos for scalp conditions. It is supposed to be safe and effective for topical use. It is said to have antibacterial, antifungal and anti-inflammatory properties. It is most commonly used for skin eruptions caused by infections such as boils or carbuncles. Along with ichthammol, drawing salve may

also contain green soap, petrolatum, beeswax, and other substances. There is antecdotal evidence that drawing salve can help bring splinters and wasp stingers to the surface of the skin. No idea if it would work on glass shrapnel."—answers.yahoo.com

[22]**Urine, medicinal effects** "For external application, new or old urine can be used. Since older urine has a higher concentration of ammonia, it is more effective against skin diseases and rashes. To make the urine old, it should be stored in a dark bottle and closed tightly and kept away from the sun for 3-4 days. A small amount of the solution is applied directly on the skin. It can also be sprayed on the skin or added to skin lotions, cream or moisturizers. Doctors advise against the use of soap immediately after applying urine on the skin

"The rationale behind urine therapy is quite simple and persuasive. Urine is believed to be a byproduct of blood filtration. It is NOT excess water that is released by the body. When blood filled with nutrients pass through the liver, the toxins are filtered out and are excreted as solid waste. The purified blood then travels to the kidney where excess nutrients are eliminated from the body. The medical name of urine is Plasma Ultrafiltrate. 95% of this liquid is water and the rest is a mixture of nutrients, urea, minerals, enzymes, antibodies and hormones.

"Urine consists of urea, which is an antifungal, antibacterial and antiviral agent. Urea is produced when the body tries to balance the ratio of sodium chloride with water. Because of its ability to kill bacteria and limit inflammation, urea is often used in ointments and lotions.

"Urine can be used internally or applied externally. For internal use, it is necessary to collect the morning's first sample. A sterile container is used, and with a dropper the patient places anywhere between 5-10 drops under his tongue. The usual system is to use 1-5 drops on the first day, followed by 5-10 drops on the second day, 5-10 drops on the morning of the third day and 5-10 drops on the evening of the third day.

"Drinking urine is a good alternative wherever water is scarce. It not only satisfies the need for liquid, but also actually keeps the body healthy. Some time ago there was an earthquake in Egypt. A survivor was pulled out of the rubble in Cairo after being trapped for three days. The man had kept himself alive by, among other things, drinking his own urine and he was in excellent condition. I heard another story about a man who kept himself alive with his own urine for a week in a collapsed mine. At the time of his rescue, he looked fine and was in extraordinary health." —health.amuchbetterway. com/urine-therapy

[23]**Worms** The worms were probably threadworms (pinworms), although there are other types of worms which can also infect the human gut. Infection with threadworms is not uncommon in children, and adults can also become infected. —netdoctor.co.uk

²⁴**Pripetchik**

A fireplace with a warming oven at top. Jewish children often sang a Yiddish song called *"Oif'n Pripetchik"* to learn their Aleph Bet. To hear this song, go to the following website:—http://www.dailymotion.com/video/x9dlve_ yiddish-song-oifen-pripetchik-aleph_ lifestyle

English Translation:
In the fireplace burns a little fire,
And the house is so nice and warm,
The rabbi teaches little children
    their aleph beis,
Remember little children,
Remember my dear little ones,
What you are learning here,
So say it again and then one more time.

A modern pripetchik

²⁵***Kaddish*** "a prayer that praises God and expresses a yearning for the establishment of God's kingdom on earth. The emotional reactions inspired by the *Kaddish* come from the circumstances in which it is said: it is recited at funerals and by mourners, and sons are required to say *Kaddish* for eleven months after the death of a parent.

"The word *Kaddish* means sanctification, and the prayer is a sanctification of God's name. *Kaddish* is only said with a *minyan* (prayer quorum of ten men), following a psalm or prayer that has been said in the presence of a minyan, since the essence of the *Kaddish* is public sanctification. The one who says *Kaddish* always stands. Whether other worshippers sit or stand depends on the congregation. It is customary for all the mourners in the congregation to recite *Kaddish* in unison. A child under the age of thirteen may say the Mourner's *Kaddish* if he has lost one of his parents. Most religious authorities allow a daughter to say *Kaddish*, although she is under no religious obligation to do so. The Mourner's *Kaddish* is recited for eleven months from the day of the death and also on the *yahrzeit* (anniversary of a death). A person may say *Kaddish* not only for parents, but also for a child, brother, or in-law. An adopted son should say it for adoptive parents who raised him. *The Rabbinical Kaddish, Half Kaddish,* and *Whole Kaddish* may be said by a *chazzan* (cantor-prayer leader) who is not a mourner and has both parents living." —jvl

²⁶**Displaced Persons Camps (DP Camps)** "Following World War II, several hundred thousand Jewish survivors remained in camps for displaced persons. The Allies established such camps in Allied-occupied Germany, Austria, and Italy for refugees waiting to leave Europe. Most Jewish DPs preferred to immigrate to Palestine but many also sought entry into the United States. They decided to remain in the DP camps until they could

leave Europe. At the end of 1946 the number of Jewish DPs was estimated at 250,000, of whom 185,000 were in Germany, 45,000 in Austria, and 20,000 in Italy. Most of the Jewish DPs were refugees from Poland, many of whom had fled the Germans into the interior of the Soviet Union during the war. Other Jewish DPs came from Czechoslovakia, Hungary, Romania, and Lithuania." —ushmm

[27]**Ziegenhain** a DP camp in the Frankfurt district of the American-occupied zone. "During the war, the camp had been a prisoner of war camp, and it later housed a TB hospital. Like many other camps, Ziegenheim [sic] had a *Talmud Torah* (religious elementary school), a synagogue, a *mikve* (Jewish ritual bath), and a kosher kitchen. The Jewish population of Ziegenhain averaged 2,020 individuals per year for 1946 and 1947. The camp closed in November 1947." —ushmm

[28]**Eschwege** "a former German air force base, in the Frankfurt district of the American-occupied zone, became a DP camp in January 1946. Eschwege Airbase housed approximately 1,770 Jews at the time of its opening and its young population quickly developed a revitalized community, evidenced by the opening of a kindergarten with fifty children by April 1947. In contrast, the elementary school had only thirty students at that time. Eschwege also had a *Talmud Torah* (religious elementary school), a *cheder* (traditional religious school for young children), and a *yeshiva* (religious academy), as well as a 'Bet Ya'akov' religious high school for girls. Religious life was also celebrated in the camp's several synagogues and *mikvah* (Jewish ritual bath). Eschwege had a sports club with 100 players, a movie theater, and a 500-seat auditorium with a theater group. The camp published the newspaper *Undzer Hofenung* (Our Hope). By October 19, 1946, Eschwege housed roughly 3,355 Jews. The camp closed on April 26, 1949." –ushmm

[29]**UNRRA** "Representatives of 44 Allied nations met in Washington, D.C., and Atlantic City in November 1943. They set up the United Nations Relief and Rehabilitation Administration (UNRRA) to provide relief to areas liberated from Axis powers after World War II. UNRRA provided billions of US dollars of rehabilitation aid, and helped about 8 million refugees. It ceased operations in the DP camps of Europe in 1947, and in Asia in 1949, upon which it ceased to exist. Its functions were transferred to several UN agencies, including the International Refugee Organization." —Britannica online and wik

[30]*Mikvah* ritual submersion in a pool. The water of the *mikveh* is designed to ritually cleanse a person. —myjewishlearning.com

[31]**The Betar Movement** (also spelled Beitar) "The name Betar stands for 'Brit Yosef Trumpeldor.' Joseph Trumpeldor was a Jewish fighter who fell, defending Tel Hai from an armed band of Arab marauders. Mortally wounded, he coined the phrase: 'Never mind, it is good to die for our [own] country.' (The name is also an allusion to the last Jewish fortress to fall during the Bar-Kochba rebellion, Betar.)

A Revisionist Zionist youth movement founded in 1923 in Riga, Latvia, by Ze'ev Jabotinsky. Betar members played important roles in the fight against the British during the Mandate, and in the creation of Israel. It has been traditionally linked to the original Herut and then Likud Israeli political parties. Most of Betar's ideology is summarized in the poem 'Shir Betar,' (The Betar Song) that Jabotinsky wrote in Paris in 1932.

In 1923, Vladimir (Ze'ev) Jabotinsky (poet, author, journalist, translator, soldier, Zionist leader) was invited to a meeting of Jewish youth in Riga, Latvia, arranged by Aaron Propes. Jabotinsky related the heroism of the one-armed Trumpeldor and of the defense, by the newly-formed *Haganah*, of Jews attacked by Arabs (tacitly supported by the British mandate authorities) in the Jerusalem Pogrom of 1920. Challenged by this Riga group to provide a blueprint for the future, Jabotinsky proposed a Zionist youth movement modeled on the ideas of courage, self-respect, military training, defense of Jewish life and property against a tide of Anti-Semitism, and settlement in Israel towards the recreation the Jewish state, as epitomized by the life of Trumpeldor. Jabotinsky also wanted to connect the name of the first proudly Jewish fighter after 2000 years to the name of the last fort of Jewish uprising against the Roman Empire in the Bar Kokhba's revolt, Betar, showing that Betar was intent to create a new generation of Jewish warriors.

"Unlike other Zionist movements, Betar focused its ideas into a single overwhelming ideal—to create that type of Jew best suited to building the state of Israel. Such a Jew needed to be 'proud, generous, and fierce'—a world away from the supposed 'ghetto' mentality of the vast majority of Jews of the time.

"Against a background of notable opposition from many quarters within the Jewish communities of Europe and the land of Israel (left-wing Zionists, anti-Zionist Bundists, assimilationists, pacifists, and many who saw Jewish militarism as either unnecessary or undesirable), Betar nevertheless quickly gained a large following in Palestine, Latvia, Lithuania, Austria, Czechoslovakia, Germany and elsewhere, but particularly in Poland, the largest centre of Jewish population in the world In 1934, Betar membership in Poland numbered over 40,000, out of a worldwide membership of 70,000. Betar organized self-defense groups in Poland to defend against attacks by the antisemitic The National Radical Camp (Polish: Obóz Narodowo Radykalny)—ONR. Routine activities in Warsaw included quasi-military drilling and instruction in Hebrew and encouraging the learning of English; the group was notable for its favorable attitude toward Mussolini for his perceived encouragement of ancient virtues among Italians and for his anti-Communism, going at one point so far as to adopt the Fascist black shirt as an unofficial uniform, but this attitude was generally reversed after the Italian invasion of Abyssinia, which was seen as cowardly.

"During the 1930s and early 40s, amid steadily increasing antisemitism in Europe and through the start of the Holocaust, with the ports of the British mandate of Palestine closed to all but a trickle of Jewish immigration,

Betar organized 'illegal' immigration to the land of Israel, secretly rescuing thousands of Jews by shipping them to Palestine and running the British blockade in barely seaworthy boats. In total, over 40,000 were saved from the Holocaust by Betar ships.

"During World War II, Betar members, including former Polish Army officers, founded *Żydowski Związek Walki* (Jewish Fighting Union) which fought in the Warsaw Ghetto Uprising. It should also be noted that Mordechai Anilewicz, the head of the other Jewish fighters in Warsaw, the Jewish Combat Organization (*Żydowska Organizacja Bojowa*, ŻOB), appears to have gained his military training in Betar, and was secretary of the massive Betar Warsaw Organization in 1938, before leaving it to join, and quickly take leadership of, the left-wing Zionist *Hashomer Hatzair* group in Warsaw. In Lithuania, unlike many areas of Europe where the local anti-Nazi partisans ignored or even slaughtered local Jews, Jewish fighters under the leadership of Yosef Glazman, head of Betar Lithuania, battled the Nazis alongside the Lithuanian partisans in the forests of Vilnius. The famous 'Song Of The Partisans,' sung as an anthem by many Holocaust survivors on *Yom HaShoah*, was written in memory of him and dedicated to him." —wik and betar.org

Joseph Trumpeldor
Hero of Tel Hai

Ze'ev Jabotinsky
Founder, Rosh Betar

[32]**International Red Cross** "an international humanitarian movement with approximately 97 million volunteers worldwide, which was started to protect human life and health, to ensure respect for the human being, and to prevent and alleviate human suffering, without any discrimination based on nationality, race, sex, religious beliefs, class or political opinions. The Red Cross and the Red Crescent have been at the service of humanity for more than a century—affording protection to those affected by conflict and to those assisting them. In December 2005, an additional emblem—the Red Crystal—was created alongside the Red Cross and the Red Crescent.

"Up until the middle of the 19th century, there were no organized and well-established army nursing systems for casualties and no safe and protected institutions to accommodate and treat those who were wounded on the battlefield. In June 1859, the Swiss businessman Henry Dunant traveled to Italy to meet French emperor Napoléon III with the intention of discussing difficulties in conducting business in Algeria, at that time occupied by France. When he arrived in the small town of Solferino on the evening of June 24, he witnessed the Battle of Solferino, an engagement in the Austro-Sardinian War. In a single day, about 40,000 soldiers on both sides died or were left wounded on the field. Henry Dunant was shocked by the terrible aftermath of the battle, the suffering of the wounded soldiers, and the near-total lack of medical attendance and basic care. He completely abandoned the original intent of his trip and for several days he devoted himself to helping with the treatment and care for the wounded. He succeeded in organizing an overwhelming level of relief assistance by motivating the local population to aid without discrimination.

"Growing from Henry Dunant's spontaneous gesture to help wounded soldiers, to become an organization reaching out to millions of war victims around the world, the ICRC has worked in most of the major crises of the past 140 years.

"Hand in hand with its operational activities have been its efforts to develop the laws governing armed conflicts, so as to ensure greater protection for those who do not, or who no longer, take part in fighting; the ICRC and the Geneva Conventions are inextricably linked.

Holocaust

"The genocide of the Jews and Gypsies and other persecutions carried out under the Third Reich were the cause of unspeakable suffering. That such events were allowed to happen is the greatest failure of Western civilization.

"This failure is also that of the Red Cross as a whole, but it weighs most heavily on the ICRC given the organization's specific mission and its position within the International Red Cross and Red Crescent Movement. Millions of men, women and children—mainly Jews, but also Gypsies, the handicapped and all those whom the regime considered as opponents or resistance fighters—were exterminated in cold blood, in atrocious conditions, without the ICRC being able to do anything to protect them. Never had the organization's guiding principles been so outrageously flouted, in a total perversion of moral values that resulted in the industrialization of death. For the survivors and the families of the victims, the wounds inflicted by these events remain open to this day.

"This failure is aggravated by the fact that the ICRC did not do everything in its power to put an end to the persecutions and help the victims. The organization remained a prisoner of its traditional procedures and of the overly narrow legal framework in which it operated. Having abandoned the idea of public condemnation – convinced as it was that this would not change the course of events, fearing that it would jeopardize the activities it was carrying out for other victims, especially prisoners of war, and not wishing to exacerbate Switzerland's relations with the belligerent States—the ICRC essentially relied on its delegates to make confidential representations to the authorities of the Reich or its satellites. However, these delegates had no access to the corridors of power. Only towards the end of the war did the ICRC's leaders make high-level representations to certain leaders of the Reich and its satellites.

"In the words of Jean-Claude Favez, who made the most thorough independent study of the ICRC's efforts to help the victims of Nazi persecution and who, to that end, was granted unlimited access to the ICRC's archives, the organization 'did not take the supreme risk of throwing the full weight of its moral authority into the scales on behalf of these particular victims.'

"Having confined itself to two options—that of the very limited aid operation it was carrying out for the victims of Nazi persecution, with derisory results in regard to the situation of the victims and no impact on the genocide, and that of public condemnation, an ultimate weapon that the ICRC felt it could not use, the organization was unable—until the last months of the war—to make determined, sustained, high-level diplomatic representations to the leaders of the Reich or to those of its allies or satellites, not all of whom shared the destructive fanaticism of Nazi dignitaries.

"Such approaches should have been attempted, even if it could be doubted that the desired results would be achieved. For if crime meets with no protest—were it only by means of confidential representations—if repeated atrocities meet with no condemnation—even if no material sanctions are imposed—then it is to be feared that the moral values underlying international humanitarian law will eventually wither away.

"With this in mind, the ICRC today regrets its past errors and omissions. This failure will remain engraved in the organization's memory, as will the brave acts undertaken by many of its delegates at the time.

"While history cannot be rewritten, the ICRC intends to honor the victims of Nazi persecution by fighting for a world in which the dignity of every man, woman and child is respected in all circumstances. 25-10-2007" — icrc.org

[33]**Soap** The story about Nazis making soap from Jewish bodies is one that has circulated for many years, especially among Holocaust survivors but also in the general population. However, recent articles, for example in *Ha'Aretz*, as well as the statements of Holocaust scholars discount this. Yehuda Bauer, distinguished Holocaust scholar and author, has said, "The story was spread as part of the Nazi campaign of psychological sadism, and very many Jews believed it in the past, and continue to believe it in the present. A type of soap that was produced by the Germans during the war was (and still is) considered to be made of human fat, and has the inscription R.I.F., which Jews erroneously interpreted as *Rein Juedisches Fett* (Pure Jewish Fat). But Juedisch is spelt with a "J" not with an "I," and the letters actually mean *Rheinlaendische Industrie Fettherstellung* (Rhineland Industrial Production). The Nazis did try to make fat from corpses, in early 1945, at an experimental station near Gdansk, out of the bodies of Polish slave laborers (not Jews). However, no industrial production was achieved, and the Soviets occupied the area in February 1945. The material was produced at the Nuremberg Trials. Had there been a Nazi industrial production of human fat, they would not have needed an experimental station." — July 10, 2006, email from Yehuda Bauer.

Michael Berenbaum, author of the *World Must Know*, concurs.

Chaim (Donald) Berkman heard and believed these stories told by adult Holocaust survivors in Eschwege DP Camp. As Yehuda Bauer has said, "Holocaust survivors were prepared to believe any horror stories about their persecutors."

[34]**Musar Movement** "a Jewish ethical, educational and cultural movement (a 'Jewish Moralist Movement') that developed in 19th century Orthodox Eastern Europe, particularly among the Lithuanian Jews. The Hebrew term *Musar* is from the book of Proverbs 1:2 meaning instruction, discipline, or conduct. The term was used by the Musar movement to refer

to disciplined efforts to further ethical and spiritual development. The study of Musar is a part of the study of Jewish ethics.

Main Elements of the Musar Ideology

"Though Salanter was not a systematic or theoretical thinker, there are a number of important points that figure strongly in his teachings:

- Talmudic study is not an end in itself. It must be accompanied by ethical study and conduct.
- It is not proper to withdraw from daily life. Religious Jews should be fully involved in the affairs of their community. (This was in contrast to precedents such as that of the Ga'on of Vilna).
- Salanter strove to create a new spiritual leadership for Jewish communities, which expressed emotional as well as intellectual qualities.
- Moralistic passages from the Bible, Rabbinic literature and medieval literature should be regularly recited in an atmosphere and tone that would affect the student emotionally.
- The student should constantly subject himself to self-examination, recording his personal shortcomings.
- Musar would inject relevance and vitality into traditional Judaism that would provide a more attractive alternative to Reform and secularism." —jvl

"The expansion of the Musar *yeshivot* continued in the period following World War II, but many of the Jews involved in the Musar movement were killed in the *Shoah*. Some, however, settled in the land of Israel and established Musar yeshivas there. While many former students of the Musar movement settled in the United States and were involved in a variety of Jewish institutions, they established no formal institutions dedicated to Musar during the 20th century.

"A recent revival of interest in the Musar movement has been underway in America in various sectors of the Jewish world. The Musar Institute, founded by Alan Morinis, and the Musar Leadership Program, founded by Rabbi Ira Stone, are among the institutions which have sought to continue the legacy of the Musar movement. Morinis' book *Everyday Holiness* and Stone's book *A Responsible Life* have been among the popular books which have sparked contemporary interest in the Musar movement." —wik

35Rabbi Israel Salanter (1810-1883)

Life

"1810--Born in Lithuania. At an early age he came under the influence of [Rabbi] Zundel, a figure who went around in common dress and placed a strong emphasis on the quality of humility. Zundel instructed Salanter to study "musar," the literature of medieval Jewish moralistic and ethical teachings.

"Salanter established his own following, and was appointed the head of a yeshivah in Vilna, where he lived in poverty. He quickly became well known in the community for his scholarship. He soon resigned this post to open up his own Yeshiva, where he emphasized moral teachings based on the ethics taught in traditional Jewish rabbinic works. He referred to his philosophy as *Musar*, Hebrew for ethics. In 1842 he established the first *Musar* society. Despite the prohibition against doing work on Shabbat (the Jewish Sabbath) Rabbi Salanter set an example for the Lithuanian Jewish community during the cholera epidemic of 1848. He made certain that any necessary relief work on *Shabbat* for Jews was done by Jews; some wanted such work to be done on Shabbat by non-Jews, but Rabbi Salanter held that both Jewish ethics and law mandated that the laws of the Torah must be put aside in order to save lives. During *Yom Kippur* (the Day of Atonement) Rabbi Salanter ordered that Jews that year must not abide by the traditional fast, but instead must eat in order to maintain their health; again for emergency health reasons. By 1850, Salanter left Vilna when he refused a Professorship in Talmud at a government-run seminary (Such institutions usually had conversionist objectives). He moved to Kovno, a known centre of reformist and enlightenment forces. Under Salanter it was transformed into a traditional Orthodox community. In Kovno Salanter established a *musar shtiebel*, a small synagogue, where ethical texts were studied. This act aroused some opposition, since it was viewed as separation from the main community.

"Later in his life, Salanter moved to Germany where he was successful in transplanting the Lithuanian 'style' of Jewish life and learning. He attempted to establish an advanced academy for married students (*kolel p'rushim*) in Berlin.

"He continued to travel through Europe fund-raising and assisting in the organization of local Jewish communities (especially in Paris)." —jvl

[36]**Chicken Farms in South Jersey** "Perhaps the most ambitious venture at creating a rural Jewish stronghold took place in southern New Jersey, where the Hirsch fund established an agricultural school, and provided start-up money for numerous chicken and egg farmers in the Woodbine and Vineland area. It was an area that, coincidentally, was looking to attract agricultural investment. Not long before the Jews started arriving, the Vineland city elders advertised in *Harper's Weekly*: 'To all wanting farms: Large and thriving settlement, mild and healthful climate, 30 miles north of Philadelphia by railroad.' It was billed as being the most 'suitable condition for pleasant farming that we know of this side of the Western prairies.' A Jewish cooperative farm settlement was started there in 1882.

"There were 3,500 Jews, mostly farmers or related to the farm industry, in the Vineland area by 1901, on land that was divided into more than 150 farms. But the difficult life led to 20 percent of the Jews dropping out by 1920. The young Jews that grew up on the farms, seeing first-hand the struggles of farming and the low economic ceiling, figured their luck couldn't be any worse in the big city. Then the Great Depression hit and there was no luck in the cities, either. Suddenly farming seemed a more certain path than the closed factories and soup lines in the city. At least you could eat the eggs.

"After World War II, a number of Holocaust survivors—most of whom had originally settled in New York—became disillusioned with life in New York. Many, with the help of HIAS and the Baron de Hirsch fund, bought chicken farms in Vineland, Millville, and Oceanville.

It was all done by hand, not by machine. You had to work seven days a week, feeding the chickens and collecting the eggs two or three times a day.' Most of the refugee farmers were poor, just a few years out of the Displaced Persons camps, and lacked the money to take on hired hands.

We had to make a living, and take care of the children, and we just did it. We were fast learners. We had to be. But in Europe we had two-dozen chickens, and we gave them corn and that was it. Here we had 5,000 chickens, sometimes 10,000. And who knew chickens got sick? Who knew chickens had to be replaced? Chickens can never lay as much as when they're young; one two winters, and after that we were feeding them for nothing.

"By the end of the 1960s, the bottom was falling out. People would listen to the radio to hear the latest price of eggs, and prices were dropping. All across America, Ma and Pa farms was being squeezed by corporate agribusiness with vast, industrialized farms, with sophisticated breeding and marketing. One by one, through the 1970s, the chicken farms closed.

Those that left the farm behind found perfectly fine Jewish communities in the big metropolitan areas, with better jobs and homes than their parents had, with wonderful synagogues and better schools, with opportunities for advancement." —www.thejewishweek.com

[37]**Harold George Belafonte, Jr.** (born March 1, 1927) a Jamaican American musician, actor and social activist. "One of the most successful popular singers in history, he was dubbed the 'King of Calypso,' a title which he was very reluctant to accept (according to the documentary Calypso Dreams) for popularizing the Caribbean musical style with an international audience in the 1950s. Belafonte is perhaps best known for singing the 'Banana Boat Song,' with its signature lyric 'Day-O.' Throughout his career, he has been an advocate for civil rights and humanitarian causes. He was a vocal critic of the policies of the George W. Bush Administration.

Belafonte (center) at the 1963 Civil Rights March on Washington, D.C., with Sidney Poitier (left), and Charlton Heston.

"Belafonte was the first black man to win an Emmy, with his first solo TV special *Tonight with Belafonte* (1959). During the 1960s he appeared in a number of TV specials, alongside such artists as Julie Andrews, Petula Clark, Lena Horne, and Nana Mouskouri. He was also a guest star on a memorable episode of *The Muppet Show* in 1978, in which he sang his signature song 'Day-O' on television for the very first time. However, the episode is best known for Belafonte singing the spiritual song, 'Turn the World Around,' that is performed with Muppets designed like African tribal masks. It has become one of the most famous performances in the series. It was reported to be Jim Henson's favorite episode, and Belafonte did a reprise of the song at Henson's funeral in 1990.

"'Turn the World Around' was also included in the 2005 official hymnal supplement of the Unitarian Universalist Association, 'Singing the Journey.' Harry Belafonte received the Kennedy Center Honors in 1989. He was awarded the National Medal of Arts in 1994 and he won a Grammy Lifetime Achievement Award in globally through the 1950s to the 2000s. He gave his last concert in 2003, and in a 2007 interview stated that he has since retired from performing."—wik

[38]**Reform Judaism** "One of the guiding principles of Reform Judaism is the autonomy of the individual. A Reform Jew has the right to decide whether to subscribe to this particular belief or to that particular practice.

"But there is a historic body of beliefs and practices that is recognized as Jewish. We Jews have survived centuries of exile and persecution as well as centuries of unparalleled spiritual and intellectual creativity because we have always thought of ourselves as a people created 'in the image of God,' dedicated to *tikkun olam*—the improvement of the world. And the particular beliefs and practices that have traditionally identified us as Jews have enabled us not only to survive creatively but to connect with the God 'who has kept us alive, sustained us, and enabled us to reach this moment.'

"Reform Jews are heirs to a vast body of beliefs and practices embodied in *Torah* and the other Jewish sacred writings. We differ from more ritually observant Jews because we recognize that our sacred heritage has evolved and adapted over the centuries and that it must continue to do so. And we also recognize that if Judaism were not capable of evolution, of Reform, it could not survive.

"Reform Judaism accepts and encourages pluralism. Judaism has never demanded uniformity of belief or practice. But we must never forget that whether we are Reform, Conservative, Reconstructionist, or Orthodox, we are all an essential part of *K'lal Yisrael*—the worldwide community of Jewry.

"All Jews have an obligation to study the traditions that have been entrusted to us and to observe those *mitzvot*--those sacred and timehallowed acts—that have meaning for us today and that can ennoble our lives, as well as those of our families and communities. It is our *mitzvoth* that put us in touch with Abraham and Sarah; with Moses, Hillel, and the Jews of fifth century Babylonia, twelfth century Spain, and eighteenth century Poland; and with the Jews of twentieth century Auschwitz, Israel, the former Soviet Union, and our neighboring town." —jvl

[39]*Kosher, or Kashrut*

- Certain animals may not be eaten at all. This restriction includes the flesh, organs, eggs and milk of the forbidden animals.
- Animals that may be eaten: any animal that has cloven hooves and chews its cud; however, any land mammal that does not have both of these qualities is forbidden, such as the pig and hare.
- Anything that has fins and scales can be eaten, but not shellfish such as lobsters, oysters, shrimp, clams and crabs.
- Birds of prey or scavengers may not be eaten.
- The birds and mammals must be killed in accordance with Jewish law.
- All blood must be drained from the meat or broiled out of it before it is eaten.
- Certain parts of permitted animals may not be eaten.
- Fruits and vegetables are permitted, but must be inspected for bugs
- Meat (the flesh of birds and mammals) cannot be eaten with dairy. Fish, eggs, fruits, vegetables and grains can be eaten with either meat or dairy. (According to some views, fish may not be eaten with meat).
- Utensils that have come into contact with meat may not be used with dairy, and vice versa. Utensils that have come into contact with non-kosher food may not be used with kosher food. This applies only where the contact occurred while the food was hot.
- Grape products made by non-Jews may not be eaten.
- There are a few other rules that are not universal.

[40]**Orthodox Judaism** "Both the Written and Oral *Torah* are of divine origin, containing the exact words of God without any human influence.

Beliefs

Rambam's 13 Principles of Faith are an excellent summary of the core beliefs of Orthodox Judaism.

- I believe with perfect faith that God is the Creator and Ruler of all things. He alone has made, does make, and will make all things.
- I believe with perfect faith that God is One. There is no unity that is in any way like His. He alone is our God. He was, He is, and He will be.
- I believe with perfect faith that God does not have a body. Physical concepts do not apply to Him. There is nothing whatsoever that resembles Him at all.
- I believe with perfect faith that God is first and last.
- I believe with perfect faith that it is only proper to pray to God. One may not pray to anyone or anything else.
- I believe with perfect faith that all the words of the prophets are true.
- I believe with perfect faith that the prophecy of Moses is absolutely true. He was the chief of all prophets, both before and after Him.
- I believe with perfect faith that the entire *Torah* that we now have is that which was given to Moses.
- I believe with perfect faith that this Torah will not be changed, and that there will never be another given by God.
- I believe with perfect faith that God knows all of man's deeds and thoughts. It is thus written (Psalm 33:15), "He has molded every heart together, and He understands what each one does."
- I believe with perfect faith that God rewards those who keep His commandments, and punishes those who transgress Him.
- I believe with perfect faith in the coming of the Messiah. How long it takes, I will await His coming every day.
- I believe with perfect faith that the dead will be brought back to life when God wills it to happen.

Practice

"In terms of practice, Orthodox Jews strictly follow the Written *Torah* and the Oral Law as interpreted by the Medieval commentators (*Rishonim*) and codified in the *Codices* (Rabbi Joseph Karo's *Shulhan Arukh* and Rabbi Moshe Isserlis's *Mapah*). From the time they get up in the morning until they go to bed at night, Orthodox Jews observe God's commandments concerning prayer, dress, food, sex, family relations, social behavior, the Sabbath day, holidays and more.

Movement

"The term 'Orthodox' Judaism only emerged as a result of the growth of new branches of Judaism. Orthodox Judaism views itself as the continuation of the beliefs and practices of normative Judaism, as accepted by the Jewish nation at Mt. Sinai and codified in successive generations in an ongoing process that continues to this day.

"It follows that Orthodox is not a unified movement with a single governing body, but rather many different movements that all strictly observe Judaism. While all orthodox movements are similar in their beliefs and observance, they differ in the details that are emphasized and in their attitudes toward modern culture and the State of Israel. Modern Orthodox tend to be a bit more liberal and more Zionistic. Ultra-Orthodox, including *Yeshivah* movements and the *Chasidic* sect, tend to be the least open to change and the most critical of modern society."—judaism.about.com

[41]**Conservative Judaism** "The roots for Conservative Judaism were laid in the Jewish Theological Seminary of America stretching back into the 1880s, but the movement was formally organized by Dr. Solomon Schechter in 1913. Dr. Schechter raised a call for unity and foresaw The United Synagogue of Conservative Jewry to be 'the greatest bequest that I shall leave to American Israel.'

"Dr. Schechter wanted the movement to implement certain key ideas: a) K'lal Yisrael (the whole of the Jewish community); b) a Jewry based on the North American experience; c) a Jewry related to modern living; d) a Jewry devoted to Torah, with education a major priority; and e) a Jewry normatively halachic.

"Conservative Judaism maintains that the truths found in Jewish scriptures and other Jewish writings come from G-d, but were transmitted by humans and contain a human component. Conservative Judaism generally accepts the binding nature of halakhah, but believes that the Law should change and adapt, absorbing aspects of the predominant culture while remaining true to Judaism's values. The idea of flexibility is deeply rooted in Conservative Judaism, and can be found within their Statement of Principles, Emet ve-Emunah.

Ismar Schorsch, Chancellor of the Jewish Theological Seminary, identifies and explores seven core values of Conservative Judaism in his monograph, 'The Sacred Cluster: The Core Values of Conservative Judaism.' According to Schorsch, the core values of Conservative Judaism are:

- The Centrality of Modern Israel
- Hebrew: The Irreplaceable Language of Jewish Expression
- Devotion to the Ideal of *Klal Yisrael*
- The Defining Role of *Torah* in the Reshaping of Judaism
- The Study of Torah
- The Governance of Jewish Life by *Halakhah*
- Belief in God

"Schorsch explains, 'Whereas other movements in modern Judaism rest on a single tenet, such as the autonomy of the individual or the inclusiveness of God's revelation at Sinai (Torah mi-Sinai), Conservative Judaism manifests a kaleidoscopic cluster of discrete and unprioritized core values. Conceptually they fall into two sets —three national and three religious — which are grounded and joined to each other by the overarching presence of God, who represents the seventh and ultimate core value.'" —judaism.about.com

Works Cited

"Belarus." Virtual Guide to Belarus. From Jan Zaprudnik. *Belarus: At the Crossroads of History.* 18 Aug. 1995. Web. 25 June 2009.

Blevett, Mary H. *Men, Women, and Work: Class, Gender, and Protest in The New England Shoe Industry 1780-1910.* Chicago: Ilini, 1990. Print.

"Druysk, Belarus." Jewish Genealogy Locality Page. 10 Aug. 2006. Web. 7 Dec. 2009.

"Eschwege." *Holocaust Encyclopedia.* United States Holocaust Memorial Museum. Web. 6 July 2009.

"Flax." Enwikipedia. Web. 21 July 2009.

Fogelman, E., and H. Bass-Wichelhaus. *Journal of Applied Psychoanalytic Studies* 4. 1, Jan. 2002: 31-47. Print.

Kasaty, Peter, ed. Natatki Z Historyji Belarusi: Ad Staradaunich Czasou Da Ciaperaszneha Momanta. Notes from *The History of Belarus: From Ancient Times to the Present Moment.* Trans. and compiled by Jauhen Reshatau. Minsk - Meadville, 1994. Trans. Dec. 1995. Apr. 1994. Web. 6 Aug. 2009.

"Kovno." *Holocaust Encyclopedia.* United States Holocaust Memorial Museum. Web. 7 July 2009.

"Lithuania." Yad Vashem. Web. 20 June 2009.

"Pearl Harbor." Pearl Harbor Raid, 7 December 1941:
        Overview and Special Image Selection. Navy History
        and Heritage Command. Web. 20 June 2009.

"Ponar." *Concise Encyclopedia of the Holocaust.*
        Yad Vashem. Web. 6 July 2009.

"Rebuilding Jewish Lives." *In Australia—Australian Memories*
        of the Holocaust. Web. 30 June 2009.

Sakowicz, Kazimierz. *Ponar Dairy 1941-1943: A Bystander's*
        Account of Mass Murder. New Haven: Yale UP, 2005. Print.

Seligman, Jon. "Holocaust in Slobodka." *History of*
        Slobodka. 2008-2009. Web. 20 June 2009.

"Soviet Union and the Eastern Front." *Holocaust*
        Encyclopedia. United States Holocaust Memorial
        Museum. Web. 6 July 2009.

"Soviet Union, Invasion of the." *Holocaust Encyclopedia.*
        United States Holocaust Memorial Museum. Web. 6
        July 2009.

"Vilna." *Holocaust Encyclopedia.* United States Holocaust
        Memorial Museum. Web. 30 Jan 2010.

Discussion Questions

—Maryann McLoughlin

Pre-reading Classroom Activities:

1. Look up "Lithuania" in the *Holocaust Encyclopedia* online at the ushmm.org website, under additional resources A-Z. Read the article, noting the dates and people involved.

2. Look up "Einsatzgruppen" in the *Holocaust Encyclopedia* online at the ushmm.org website, under additional resources A-Z. Read the article, noting the dates and people involved.

3. Look at the maps at the beginning of the book. What do you notice about the third map? Look at it closely and read the description under the map before answering.

4. Make a list of the words you did not know. Are these words explained for you in the Endnotes? If not, look them up.

Reading Activities:

1. List the people who are mentioned in the memoir. Can you describe them?

2. How is the book organized? Explain.

3. Why is the book titled *Two Voices*? Explain.

4. Why did Sara, Don, Michel, Sarah Tsipa, and Zelda leave Druysk?

5. How was shoemaking in Lithuania and Poland different from present day shoemaking in the United States?

6. Make a timeline from the beginning of Sara's life to the end of this memoir Include the important events in Sara's life.

7. Make a timeline from the beginning of Donald's life to the end of his memoir Include the important events in Don's life.

8. Discuss the significance of family to Don.

9. Discuss the significance of religion to Don?

10. Discuss the signficance of education to Don.

11. Symbols are objects that stand for or represent something else. Explain the symbolism (what they represent or stand for) of the knitting needles, the *pripetchik*, Babi Yar, potatoes, milk, donuts, gold coins, chicken farms, and cheeseburger.

12. Describe two of the photographs. Do you have photographs similar (not the same) to these in your family album?

Post-reading Classroom Activities:

1. Using the chart below, prepare an identity chart for yourself. Consider all the factors—family, school, hobbies, nationality, ethnicity, religion, etc.—that influence how you think about yourself and make decisions.

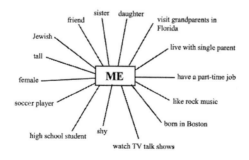

Sample Chart

2. Prepare identity charts for Sara Berkman Chipkin and Donald Berkman. Make sure to include influences before, during, and after World War II and the Holocaust (*Shoah*).

3. Write a letter to the author, commenting on his book and/or asking him questions.

4. Write a letter to the author, asking him to come speak with your class. Prepare three questions that you would ask him.

5. Have a "Donald Berkman" in your school. Teach the other classes at your grade level about Mr. Berkman, his childhood in the forest, his life in the DP Camps, and immigration to the U.S, as well as his schooling in South Jersey. Make posters and/or power points to educate the other grades. Invite Donald Berkman to an assembly for all the students in your grade.

For Further Reflection:

1. According to the scholar Samantha Power, an *upstander* is an individual who takes risks to help others in danger and does not hesitate to criticize those who fail to help others in need or danger. Describe the upstanders in *Two Voices*? Do you know any upstanders? What is the opposite of an upstander? Are there any bystanders in the book?

2. Think about historical events that have intersected with and influenced your life. Discuss these.

3. Discuss how silence and indifference to the human and civil rights of the Jews helped the perpetrators.

4. What are the obligations of responsible citizens in a democratic society?